# CUT AND CREATE!

## ABC

### EASY STEP-BY-STEP PROJECTS THAT TEACH SCISSOR SKILLS

**Written and illustrated by Kim Rankin**

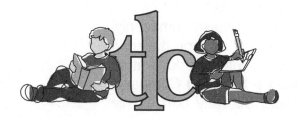

## Teaching & Learning Company

1204 Buchanan St., P.O. Box 10
Carthage, IL 62321-0010

# This book belongs to

_____

Cover by Kim Rankin

Copyright © 1998, Teaching & Learning Company

ISBN No. 1-57310-114-1

Printing No. 9876

**Teaching & Learning Company**
**1204 Buchanan St., P.O. Box 10**
**Carthage, IL  62321-0010**

# TABLE OF CONTENTS

# Dear Teacher or Parent,

"I did it myself" is a phrase which can be the foundation for a lifetime of accomplishment and positive self-esteem.

*Cut and Create* activities can be used by the teacher or parent to develop a variety of important early skills and to provide projects in which children can take pride and succeed.

- Simple patterns and easy, step-by-step directions develop scissor skills and give practice in visual-motor coordination. The scissor rating system in the upper right-hand corner on the first page of each project quickly identifies the easiest projects (✂), moderate (✂ ✂) and challenging (✂ ✂ ✂).
- Materials used are inexpensive and readily available.
- Finished products are fun, colorful and have myriad uses from play items to props; room decorations for walls, bulletin boards or mobiles; learning center manipulatives for counting, sorting, classifying or labeling; gifts or favors for parties or guests; and much more.

The simple and fun activities included in this book will help young learners build a solid base for a variety of skills such as: following directions, observation, discrimination and information processing. Various learning styles are addressed including visual, auditory and tactile.

Your art program, whether structured or serendipitous, can benefit from these simple and sequenced scissor skill activities. Your students will

- develop manual dexterity
- communicate
- learn to control his or her environment by being responsible for tools and materials
- observe
- discriminate (by color, shape, texture)
- sort, order, group and engage in other math processes
- imagine!

We hope you and your students will enjoy these projects. They have been designed to stimulate learning and creativity in a way that is simple and fun. So go cut and create! And have a good time!

Sincerely,

*Kim*

Kim Rankin

# SUGGESTIONS FOR USING SOME OF THE PROJECTS

## Greeting Cards

Celebrate a holiday or create an occasion. Handmade greeting cards are a surefire hit for parents, grandparents, relatives and friends. And what better way to say "thank you" to a visitor, custodian, principal, helper, etc.

## Flannel Board Figures

Cut figures from flannel instead of paper or glue a piece of flannel or sandpaper to the back of the finished paper figure.

## Bulletin Boards

Use completed projects to create a variety of bulletin boards throughout the year. For example, the camera (page 12) could be displayed with photographs of each of your students for a getting-to-know-you or parents' night board. Use the house (page 25), igloo (page 27), nest (page 37) and tepee (page 55) for a "Who Lives Here?" display. Or use the kite (page 31), rainbow (page 47), umbrella (page 57) and violet (page 59) to welcome spring.

## Different Uses

- Bulletin Boards
- Ceiling Decorations
- Flannel Board Figures
- Greeting Cards (Reduce 30-40%)
- Mobiles
- Paper Bag Puppets
- Party Favors
- Rebus Stories
- Refrigerator Magnets (Reduce 25-40%)
- Stick Puppets/Finger Puppets
- Tabletop or Desk Decorations
- Take-Homes for Parents
- Window/Door Decorations
- Portfolio Pieces
- Folders (Reduce 30-50%)

Create this bulletin board using the moon (page 35), nest (page 37), owl (page 39), corrugated cardboard tree and student pictures.

## Mobiles

Here are two suggestions for making a mobile. One way is to use a sturdy paper plate for the top piece. Punch holes around the outer edge of the plate. Use string or yarn in random lengths to attach the ready-made patterns to the top piece.

Another way is to use sturdy tagboard. Cut a rectangle shape approximately 3" x 32" (8 x 56 cm) and staple the ends together to form a circle. Punch holes around the bottom edge. Use string or yarn in random lengths to attach the ready-made patterns. (Note: You will have to reduce the patterns 40 to 50% so they are not too big for the mobile.)

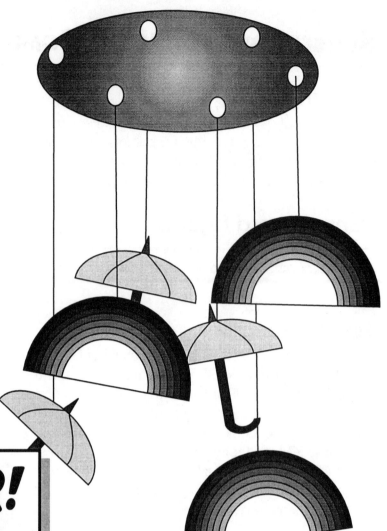

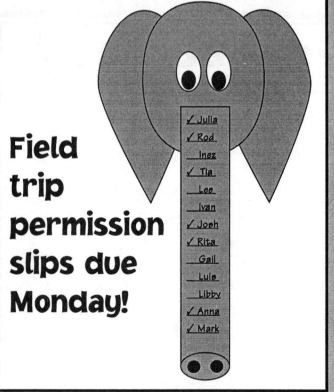

**REMEMBER!**

**Field trip permission slips due Monday!**

✓ Julia
✓ Rod
Inez
✓ Tia
Lee
Ivan
✓ Josh
✓ Rita
Gail
Lula
Libby
✓ Anna
✓ Mark

## Window/Door Decorations

Attach figures to door or window for a welcome-to-school, parent conference or special occasion display. Add extra pieces, if required. (Shown here: enlarged elephant [page 17] with extra-long trunk for recording student names.)

**Materials:** *black, brown, green, light yellow, red and white paper; scissors; glue; black crayon or marker*
**Optional Materials:** *apple seeds*

# A IS FOR APPLE

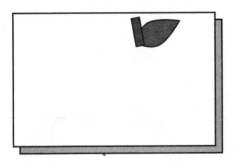

**1** Cut one #1 leaf from green paper. Cut one #2 stem from brown paper. Glue the leaf to a sheet of construction paper. Glue the stem on top of the leaf, as shown.

**2** Cut one #3 apple from red paper and glue the apple on top of the stem and leaf, as shown.

**3** Cut one #4 apple half from red paper and glue to the front of the apple as shown.

**4** Cut one #5 apple center from white paper and glue to the front of the apple half as shown.

**5** Cut one #6 core from light yellow or white paper and glue to the apple half as shown. Cut two #7 seeds from black paper and glue to the core. Cut one #8 shine from white paper and glue as shown.

**6** Cut letters *Aa* from construction paper or use the letter patterns in the back of the book. Glue the letters as shown.

**Note:** You could use real apple seeds in place of piece #7.

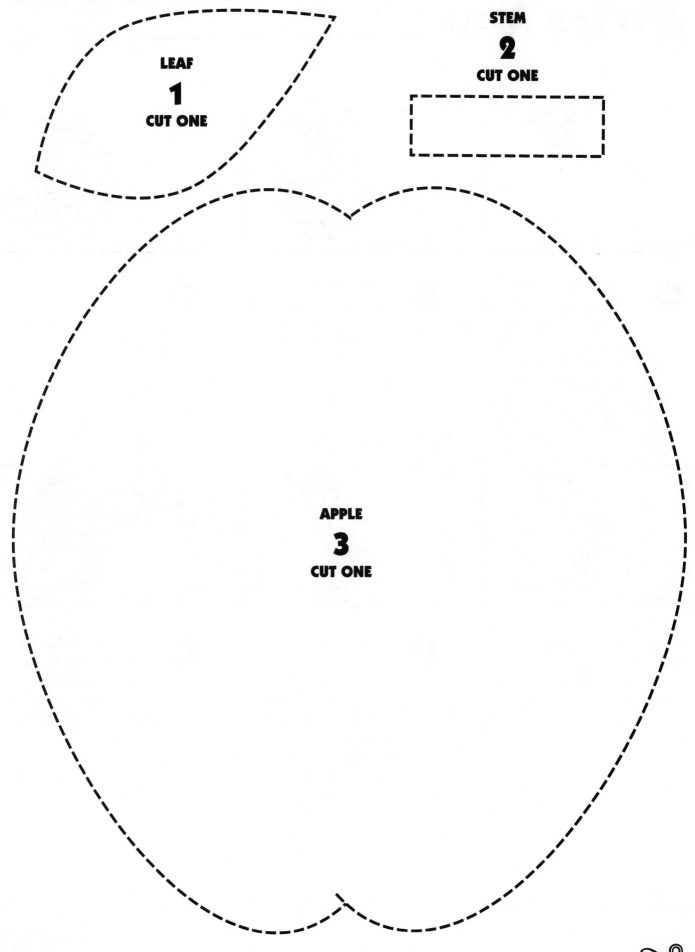

**A is for Apple**

LEAF

**1**

CUT ONE

STEM

**2**

CUT ONE

APPLE

**3**

CUT ONE

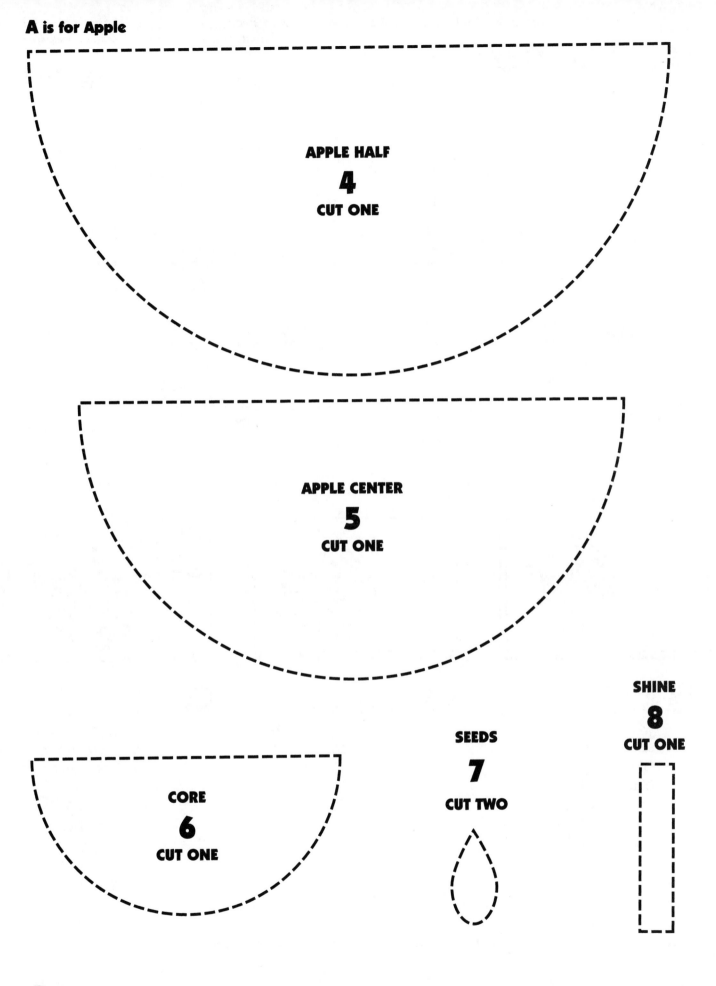

**APPLE HALF**

**4**

**CUT ONE**

**APPLE CENTER**

**5**

**CUT ONE**

**SHINE**

**8**

**CUT ONE**

**CORE**

**6**

**CUT ONE**

**SEEDS**

**7**

**CUT TWO**

# B IS FOR BABY

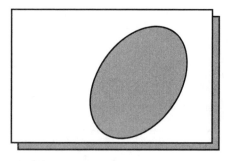

**1** Cut one #1 body from pink or blue paper. Glue to a sheet of construction paper.

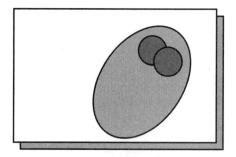

**2** Cut two #2 collars from whatever color collar you desire. Glue the two collars together and glue to the body as shown.

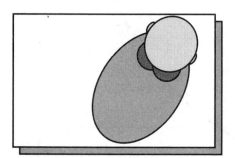

**3** Cut one #3 head from flesh-colored paper. Cut two #4 ears from the same color of paper. Glue the ears to the back of the head. Then glue the head piece to the top of the collar and body as shown.

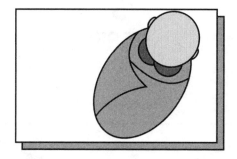

**4** Use a black crayon or marker to make the baby look like its in a blanket as illustrated.

**5** Cut two #5 hands from flesh-colored paper and glue over the lines you drew. Draw on the baby's face with a black crayon or marker. Cut the letters *Bb* from construction paper or use the patterns in the back of the book. Glue the letters as shown.

**Note:** You can use fabric, gift wrap or wallpaper for the body and collar pieces.

**B is for Baby**

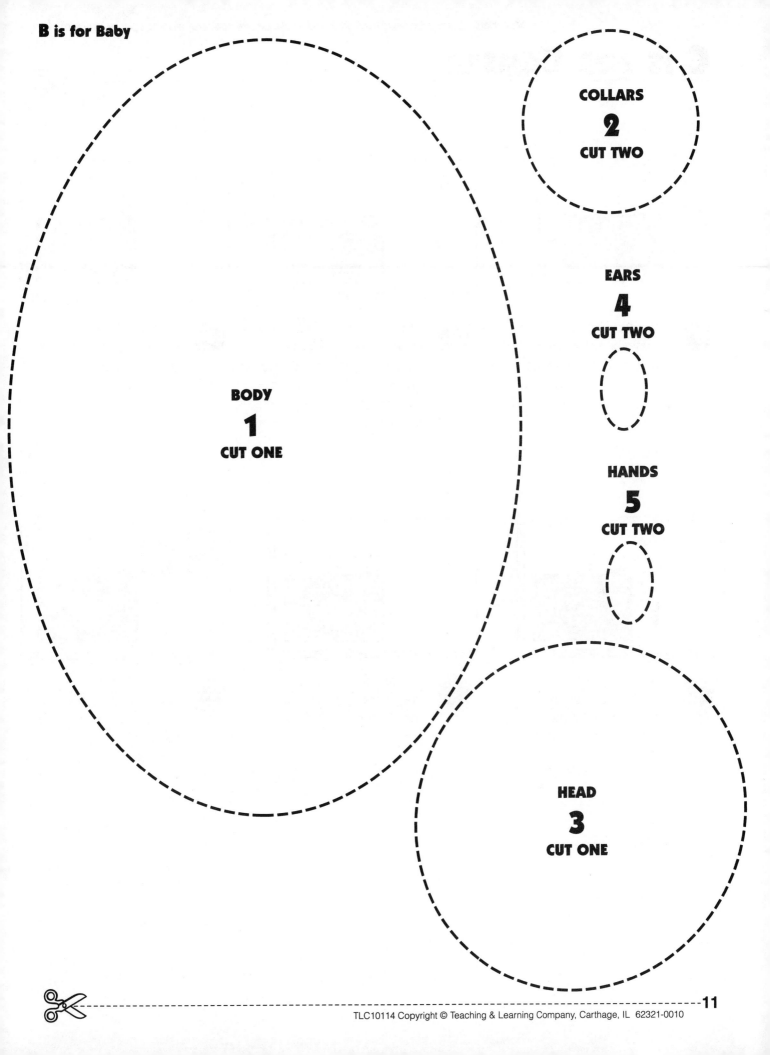

COLLARS
**2**
CUT TWO

EARS
**4**
CUT TWO

HANDS
**5**
CUT TWO

BODY
**1**
CUT ONE

HEAD
**3**
CUT ONE

# C IS FOR CAMERA

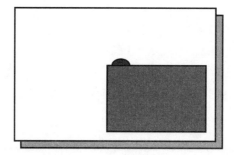

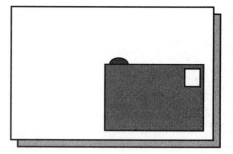

**1** Cut one #1 camera from whatever color you choose for the camera.

**2** Cut one #2 button from a darker color. Glue the button to the back of the camera as shown. Glue to a sheet of construction paper.

**3** Cut one #3 flash from white paper and glue in the corner of the camera, as shown.

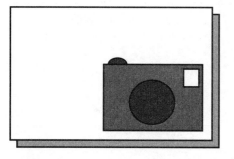

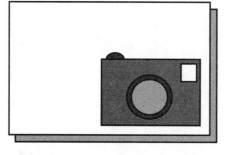

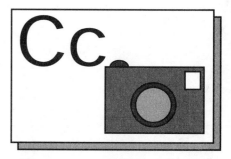

**4** Cut one #4 lens from a dark gray paper and glue in the center of the camera.

**5** Cut one #5 lens from gray paper and glue to the center of the larger lens.

**6** Cut the letters *Cc* from construction paper or use the patterns in the back of the book. Glue the letters as shown.

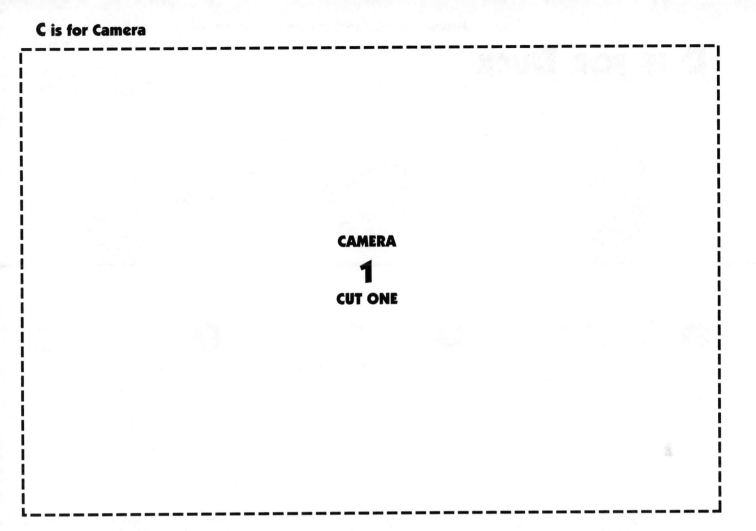

CAMERA

**1**

CUT ONE

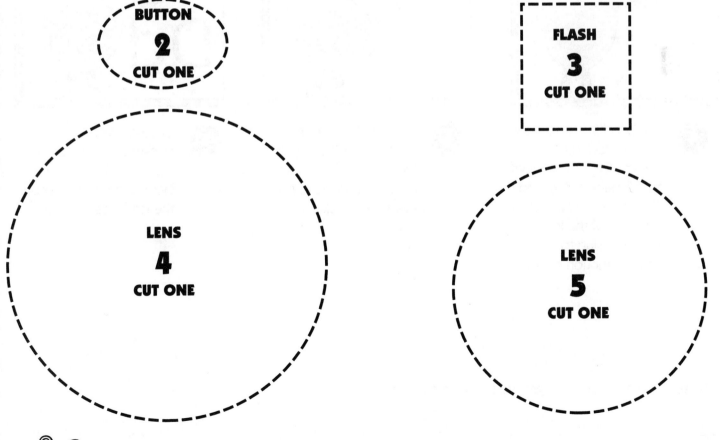

BUTTON

**2**

CUT ONE

FLASH

**3**

CUT ONE

LENS

**4**

CUT ONE

LENS

**5**

CUT ONE

**Materials:** *black, orange and yellow paper; scissors; glue; black crayon or marker*
**Optional Materials:** *wiggly eyes*

# D IS FOR DUCK

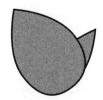

**1** Cut one #1 body from yellow paper.

**2** Cut one #2 tail from yellow paper and glue to the back of the body as shown.

**3** Cut one #3 head from yellow paper. Cut two #4 bills from orange paper and glue to the back of the head. Then glue the head to the body as shown.

**4** Cut two #5 legs and two #6 feet from orange paper. Glue the #5 legs to the back of the body. Then glue the #6 feet to the tops of the legs as shown. Glue to a sheet of construction paper.

**5** Cut one #7 wing from yellow paper and glue to the top of the body as shown. Cut one #8 eye from black paper and glue to the head as illustrated.

**6** Cut the letters *Dd* from construction paper or use the patterns in the back of the book. Glue the letters as shown.

**Note:** You may use a wiggly eye for pattern piece #8.

**D is for Duck**

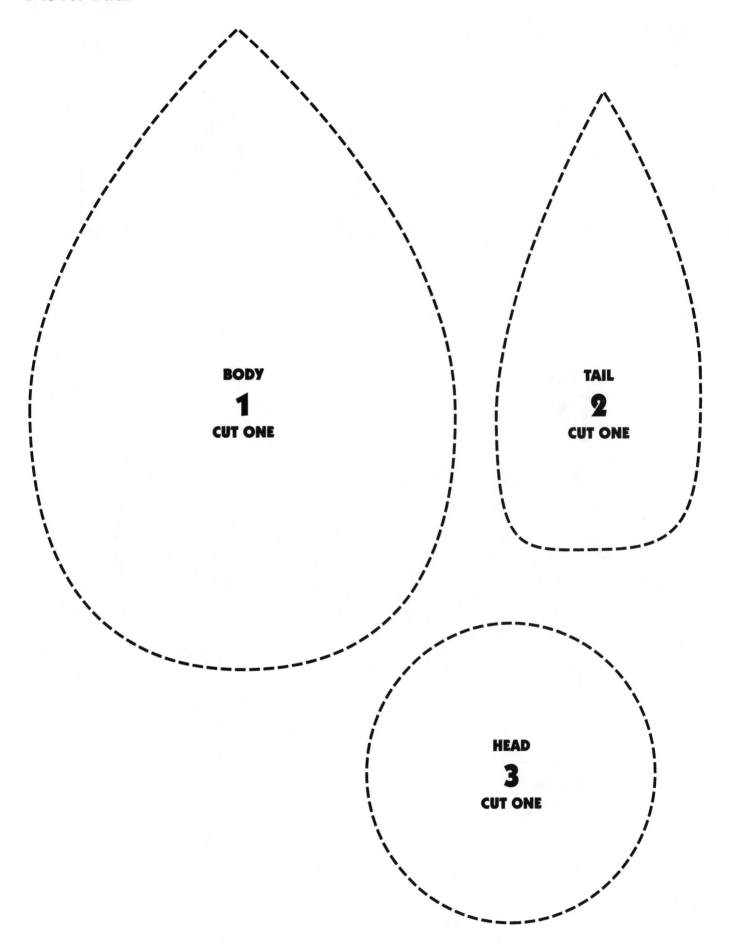

BODY

**1**

CUT ONE

TAIL

**2**

CUT ONE

HEAD

**3**

CUT ONE

**BILLS**

**4**

**CUT TWO**

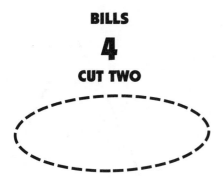

**LEGS**

**5**

**CUT TWO**

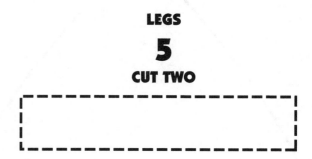

**FEET**

**6**

**CUT TWO**

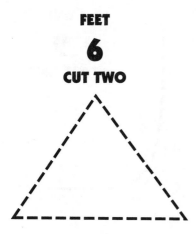

**WING**

**7**

**CUT ONE**

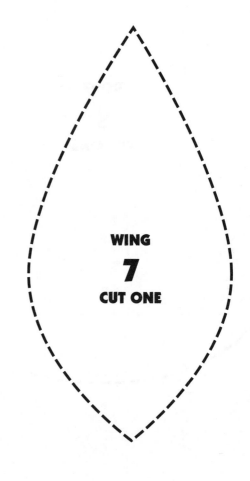

**EYE**

**8**

**CUT ONE**

**Materials:** *black, blue, brown, flesh-colored, gray and white paper; scissors; glue; black crayon or marker*

# E IS FOR ELEPHANT

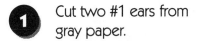

**1** Cut two #1 ears from gray paper.

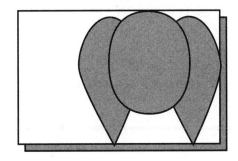

**2** Cut one #2 head from gray paper. Glue the ears to the back of the head as shown. Glue to a sheet of construction paper.

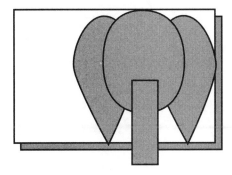

**3** Cut one #3 trunk from gray paper and glue on the front of the head as illustrated.

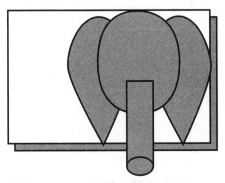

**4** Cut one #4 nose from gray paper and glue to the end of the trunk.

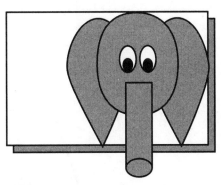

**5** Cut two #5 eyes from white paper and two #6 pupils from black paper. Glue the pupils to the eyes. Then glue to the head as shown. You may draw on the eyes with a black crayon or marker.

**6** Cut two #7 nostrils from black paper and glue on the end of the nose. Cut the letters *Ee* from construction paper or use the patterns in the back of the book. Glue the letters as shown.

**Note:** Cut the trunk extra-long and use as shown on page 6.

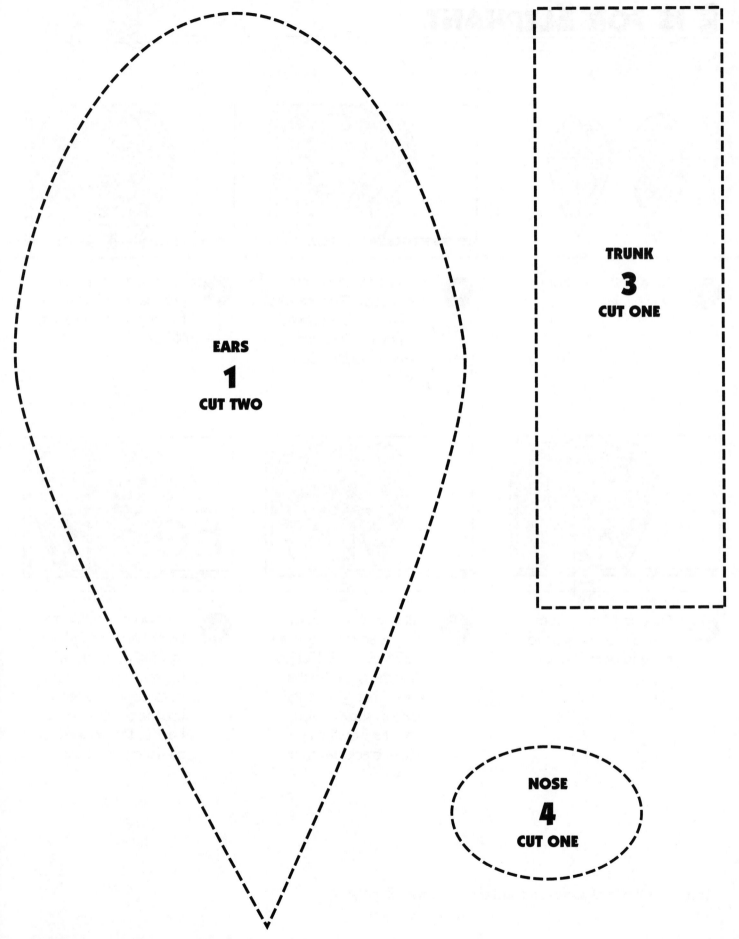

EARS

**1**

CUT TWO

TRUNK

**3**

CUT ONE

NOSE

**4**

CUT ONE

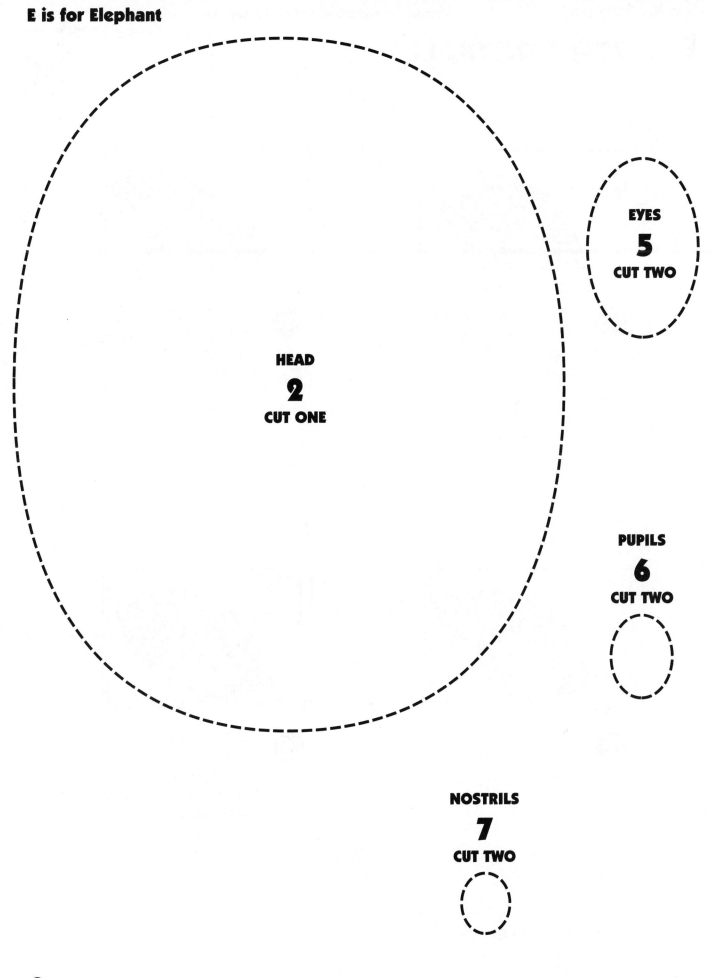

**EYES**
**5**
**CUT TWO**

**HEAD**
**2**
**CUT ONE**

**PUPILS**
**6**
**CUT TWO**

**NOSTRILS**
**7**
**CUT TWO**

**Materials:** *black, brown and white paper; scissors; glue; black crayon or marker*
**Optional Materials:** *yarn*

# F IS FOR FOOTBALL

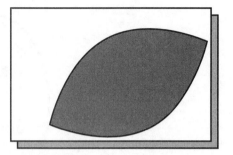

**1** Cut one #1 football from brown paper. Glue to a sheet of construction paper.

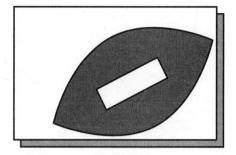

**2** Cut one #2 strip from white paper and glue in the middle of the football.

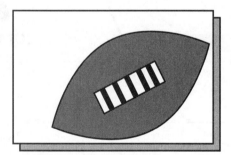

**3** Cut five #3 laces from black paper and glue as shown.

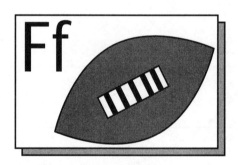

**4** Cut the letters *Ff* from construction paper or use the patterns in the back of the book. Glue the letters as shown.

**Note:** You can use yarn for the laces.

**F is for Football**

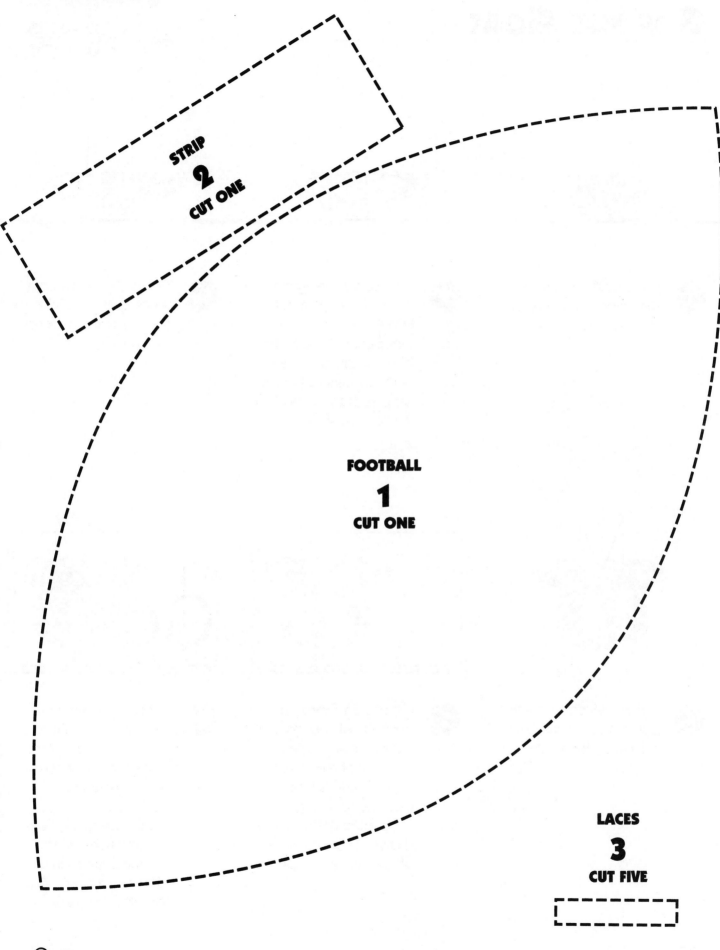

STRIP
**2**
CUT ONE

FOOTBALL
**1**
CUT ONE

LACES
**3**
CUT FIVE

**Materials:** black, brown, green, light yellow, red and white paper; scissors; glue; black crayon or marker

# G IS FOR GOAT

**1** Cut one #1 head from the color of your choice for your goat.

**2** Cut two #2 ears from the color of your goat. Cut two #3 inner ears from pink paper. Glue to the #3 inner ears to the top of the #2 ears. Glue the ear pieces to the back of the head as shown.

**3** Cut two #4 horns from white paper and glue to the top of the back of the head.

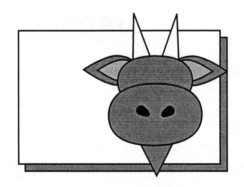

**4** Cut one #5 chin from the color of your goat. Glue on top of the head as shown.

**5** Cut one #6 beard from the color of your goat or a darker color. Glue to the back of the chin. Cut two #7 nostrils from black paper and glue in the middle of the chin as shown. Glue to a sheet of construction paper.

**6** Cut two #8 eyes from black paper and glue on the head. Use a black marker or crayon to draw on the mouth as illustrated.
Cut the letters *Gg* from construction paper or use the patterns in the back of the book. Glue the letters as shown.

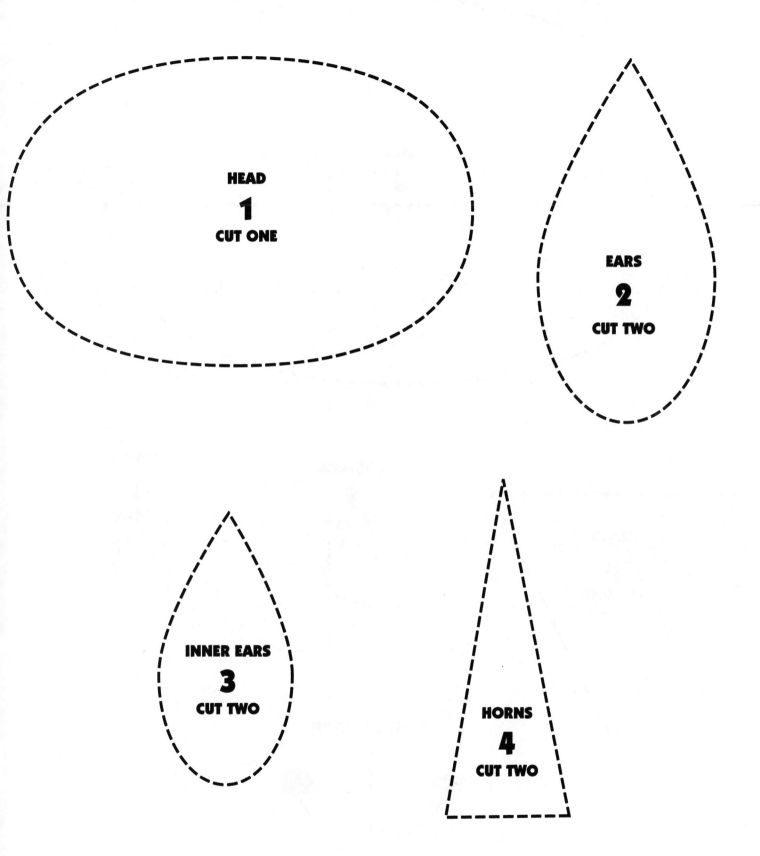

HEAD
**1**
CUT ONE

EARS
**2**
CUT TWO

INNER EARS
**3**
CUT TWO

HORNS
**4**
CUT TWO

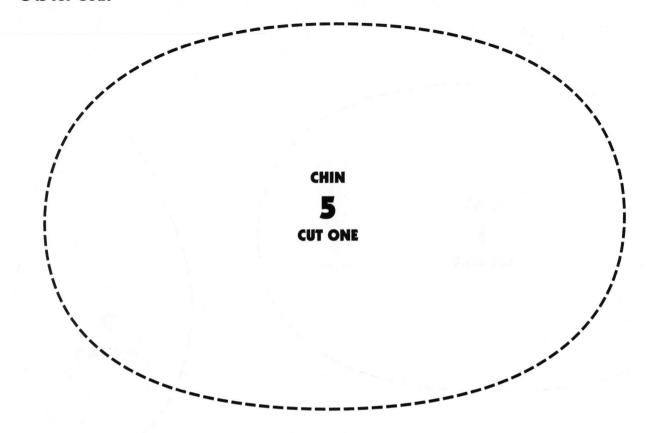

**CHIN**

# 5

**CUT ONE**

**NOSTRILS**

# 7

**CUT TWO**

**EYES**

# 8

**CUT TWO**

**BEARD**

# 6

**CUT ONE**

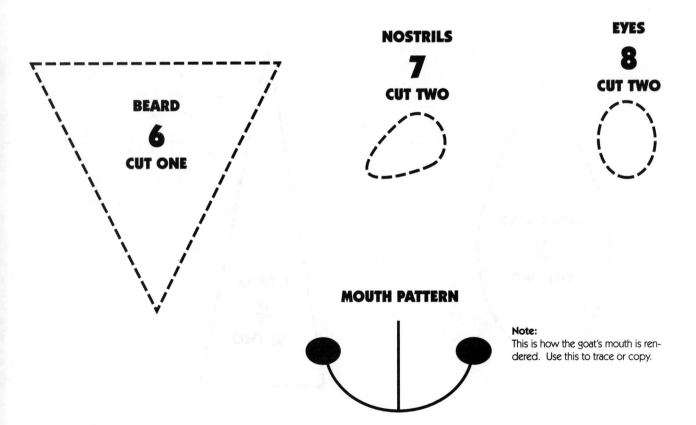

**MOUTH PATTERN**

**Note:**
This is how the goat's mouth is rendered. Use this to trace or copy.

# H IS FOR HOUSE

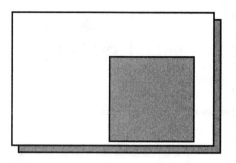

**1** Cut one #1 house from a color you choose. Glue to a sheet of construction paper.

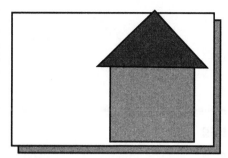

**2** Cut one #2 roof from gray paper.

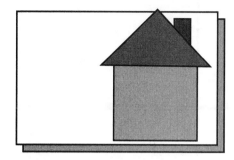

**3** Cut one #3 chimney from red or brown paper. Glue the chimney to the back of the roof as shown. Glue the roof to the top of the house.

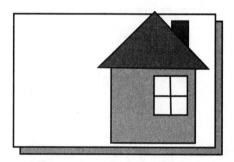

**4** Cut one #4 window from white paper and glue to the house as illustrated. Draw lines to create the windows with a black crayon or marker.

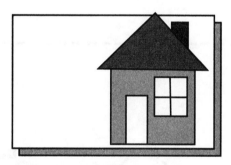

**5** Cut one #5 door from white paper or your choice of color. Glue on the door as shown.

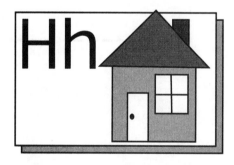

**6** Cut one #6 doorknob from black paper and glue in place as shown or use a marker to draw on a doorknob.
Cut the letters *Hh* from construction paper or use the patterns in the back of the book. Glue the letters as shown.

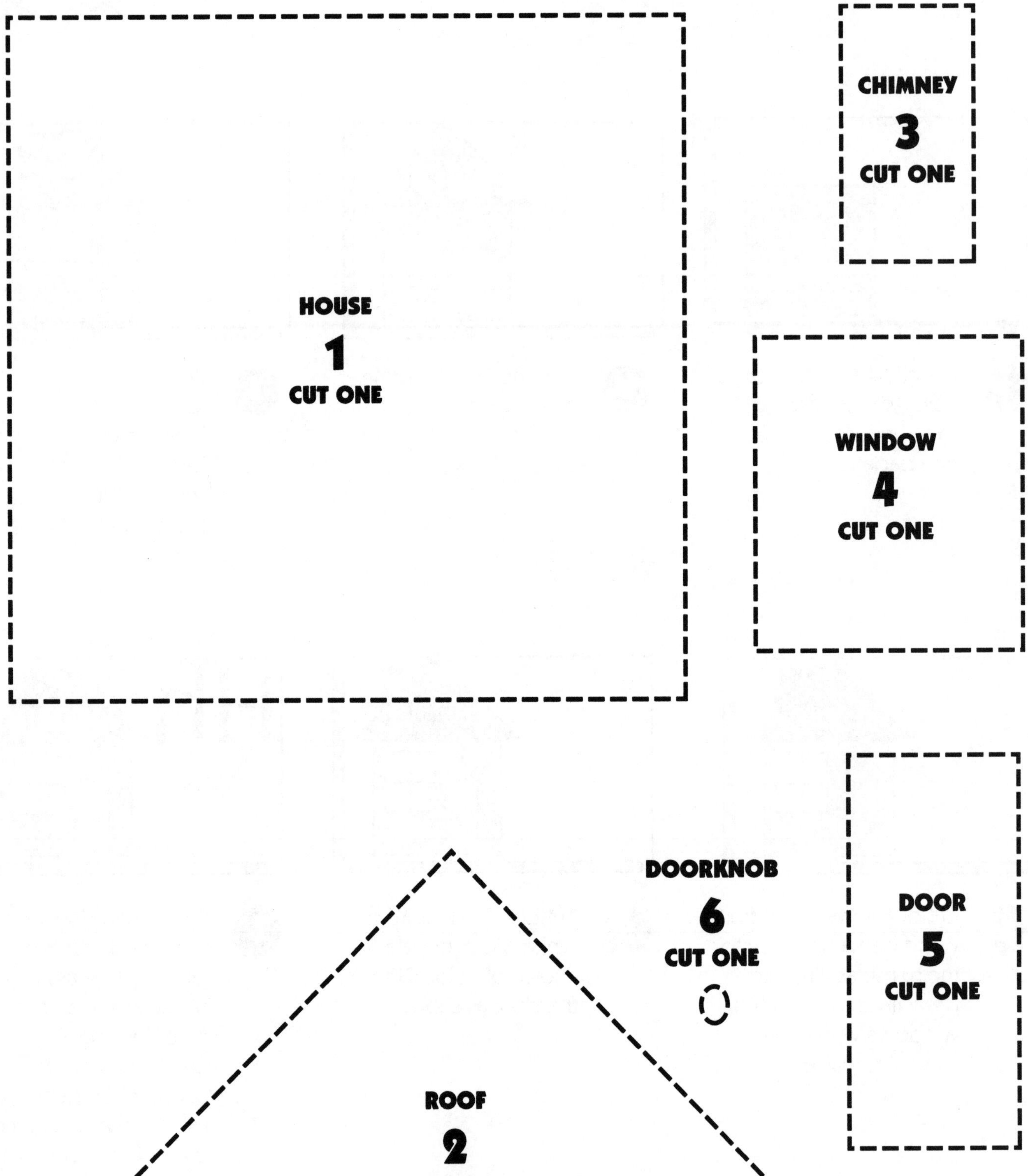

CHIMNEY

**3**

CUT ONE

HOUSE

**1**

CUT ONE

WINDOW

**4**

CUT ONE

DOORKNOB

**6**

CUT ONE

DOOR

**5**

CUT ONE

ROOF

**2**

CUT ONE

**Materials:** *light blue and white paper; scissors; glue; black crayon or marker*

# I IS FOR IGLOO

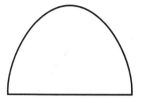

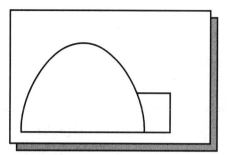

**1** Cut one #1 igloo from white paper.

**2** Cut one #2 side door from white paper. Glue to the back of the igloo. Glue to a sheet of construction paper.

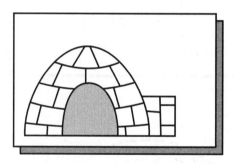

**3** Cut one #3 door from light blue paper. Glue to the front of the igloo as shown. Use a black marker or crayon to draw lines to make the blocks on the igloo as illustrated.

**4** Cut the letters *Ii* from construction paper or use the patterns in the back of the book. Glue the letters as shown.

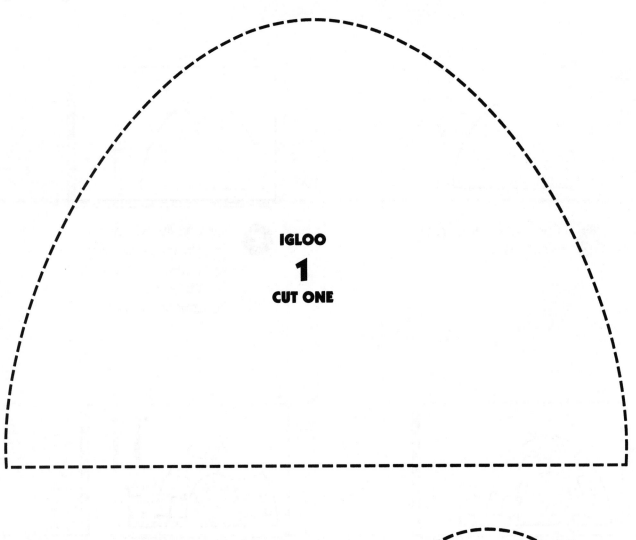

**IGLOO**

**1**

**CUT ONE**

**SIDE DOOR**

**2**

**CUT ONE**

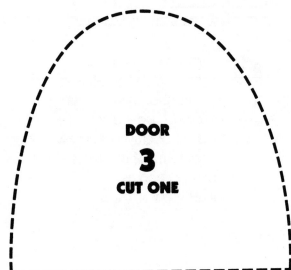

**DOOR**

**3**

**CUT ONE**

**Materials:** black, blue, light blue, orange, red, yellow and white paper; scissors; glue; black crayon or marker

**Optional Materials:** wiggly eyes and yarn

# J IS FOR JACK-IN-THE-BOX

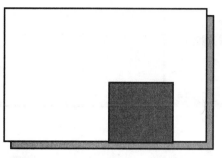

**1** Cut one #1 box from red paper. Glue to a sheet of construction paper.

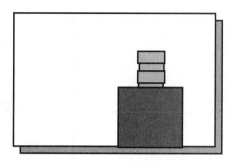

**2** Cut four #2 springs and three #3 springs from blue paper. Glue alternating one on top of the other. Then glue to the box as shown.

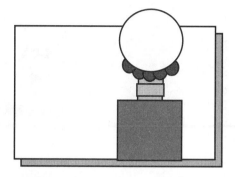

**3** Cut five #4 ruffles from light blue paper. Cut one #5 head from white paper. Overlap the ruffles gluing them to the back of the head as shown.

**4** Cut two #6 ears from white paper and glue to the back of the head as shown. Cut three #7 hairs from orange paper and glue to the back of the head. Glue the head to the springs as illustrated.

**5** Cut two #8 eyes from yellow paper and glue on the head. Cut two #9 pupils from black paper and glue in the center of eyes or use a black marker or crayon to draw the pupils.
Cut one #10 nose from red paper and glue in place as shown.

**6** Use a black marker or crayon to draw on the mouth. Cut one #11 tongue from red paper and glue in place as shown.
Cut the letters *Jj* from construction paper or use the patterns in the back of the book. Glue the letters as shown.

**Note:** You may use wiggly eyes or add yarn for hair.

TLC10114 Copyright © Teaching & Learning Company, Carthage, IL 62321-0010

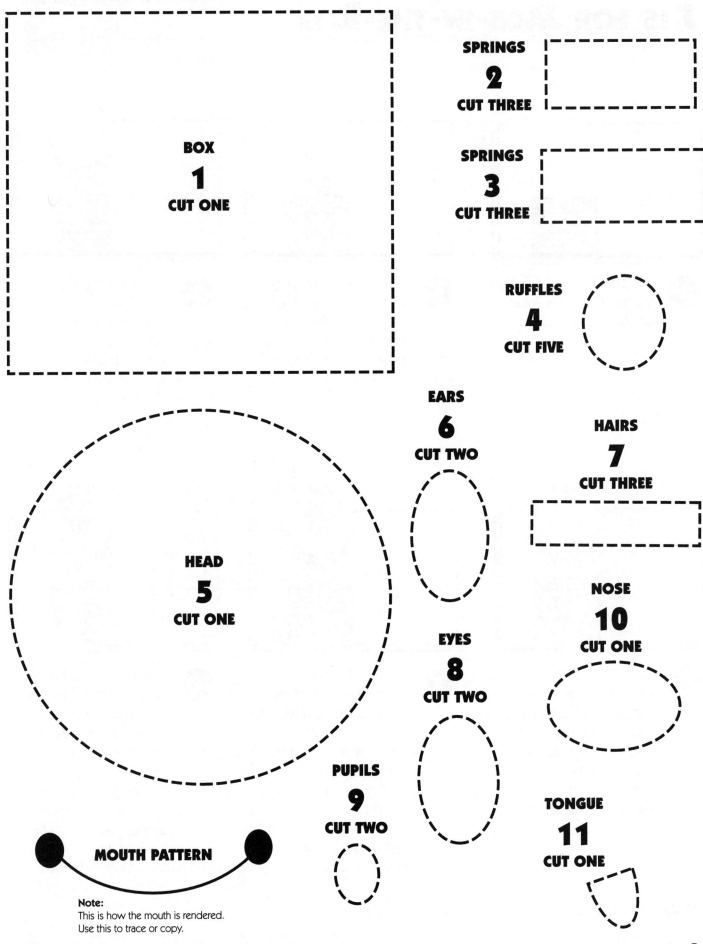

**BOX**
**1**
**CUT ONE**

**SPRINGS**
**2**
**CUT THREE**

**SPRINGS**
**3**
**CUT THREE**

**RUFFLES**
**4**
**CUT FIVE**

**EARS**
**6**
**CUT TWO**

**HAIRS**
**7**
**CUT THREE**

**HEAD**
**5**
**CUT ONE**

**NOSE**
**10**
**CUT ONE**

**EYES**
**8**
**CUT TWO**

**PUPILS**
**9**
**CUT TWO**

**TONGUE**
**11**
**CUT ONE**

**MOUTH PATTERN**

**Note:**
This is how the mouth is rendered.
Use this to trace or copy.

**Materials:** *red and a variety of colors of paper; scissors; glue; black crayon or marker*

**Optional Materials:** *yarn*

# K IS FOR KITE

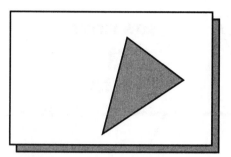

**1** Cut one #1 kite from a color of your choice. Glue to a sheet of construction paper.

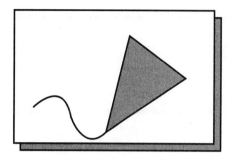

**2** Use a black crayon or marker to draw on a tail or cut a piece of yarn for the tail.

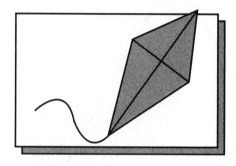

**3** Cut one #2 top from the color of your kite and glue to the kite. Use a black crayon or marker to draw a line down the center of the kite as shown.

**4** Cut six #3 bow pieces from red paper. Glue two bow pieces together as illustrated. Then glue the bows to the kite string. Cut the letters *Kk* from construction paper or use the patterns in the back of the book. Glue the letters as shown.

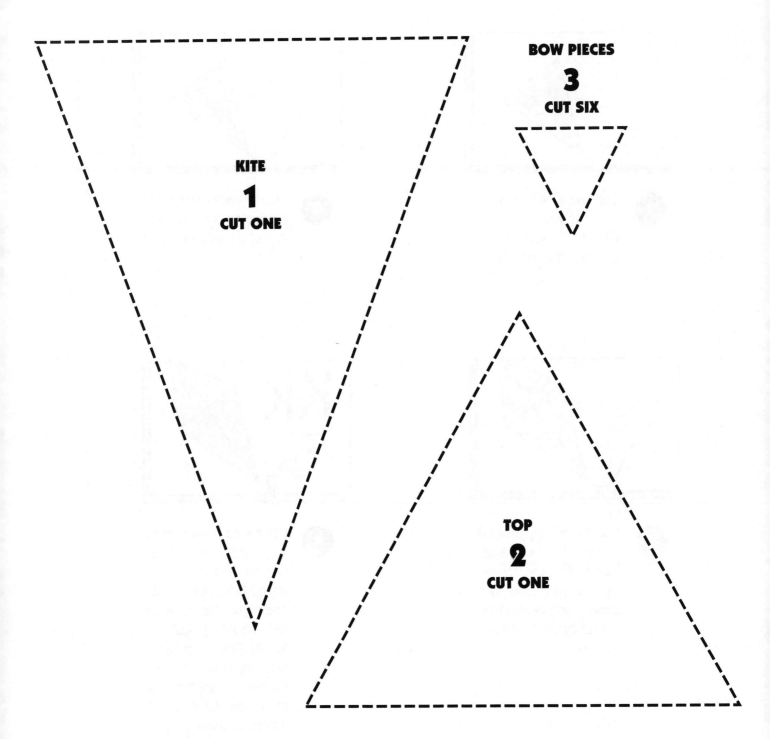

**BOW PIECES**
**3**
**CUT SIX**

**KITE**
**1**
**CUT ONE**

**TOP**
**2**
**CUT ONE**

**Materials:** *brown and a variety of colors of paper; scissors; glue; black crayon or marker*
**Optional Materials:** *craft sticks*

# L IS FOR LOLLIPOPS

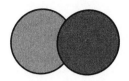

**1** Cut two #1 lollipops from your choice of colors.

**2** Cut two #2 sticks from brown paper or use craft sticks.

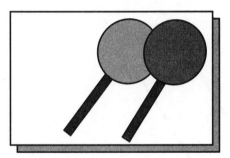

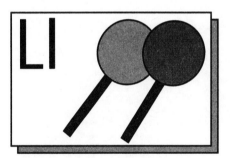

**3** Glue a stick to the back of each lollipop. Then glue the lollipops to a sheet of construction paper.

**4** Cut the letters *Ll* from construction paper or use the patterns in the back of the book. Glue the letters as shown.

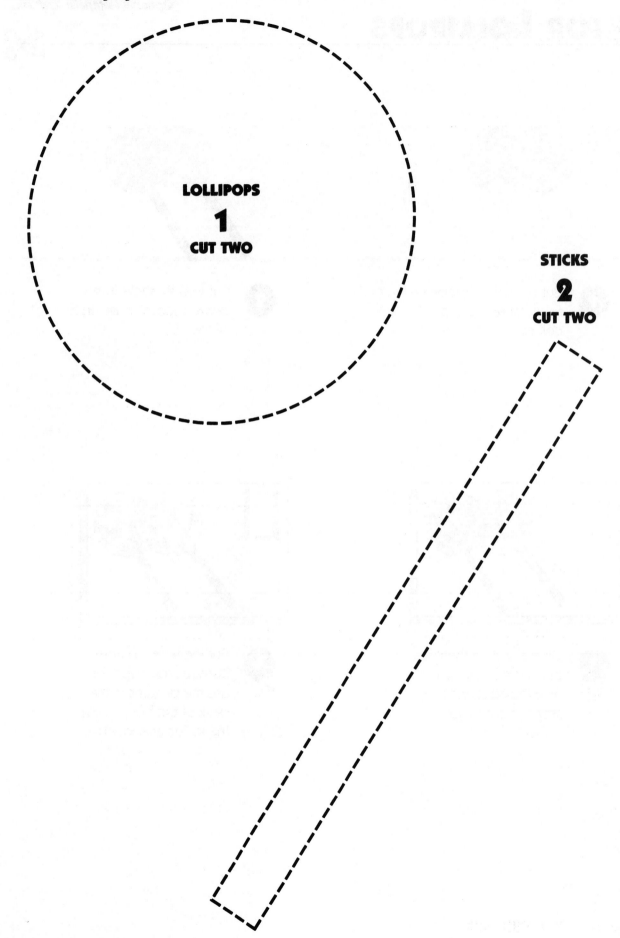

**LOLLIPOPS**

# 1

**CUT TWO**

**STICKS**

# 2

**CUT TWO**

# M IS FOR MOON

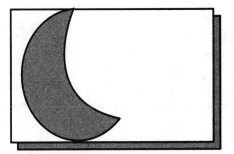

**1** Cut one #1 moon from yellow paper. Glue to a sheet of construction paper.

**2** Cut one #2 eye from white paper. Cut one #3 pupil from black paper or use a black crayon or marker to draw on the pupil. Glue the eye to the moon as shown.

**3** Cut one #4 nose from yellow paper and glue in place.

**4** Draw on the mouth with a black crayon or marker as illustrated.
Cut the letters *Mm* from construction paper or use the patterns in the back of the book. Glue the letters as shown.

**Note:** You can use a wiggly eye.

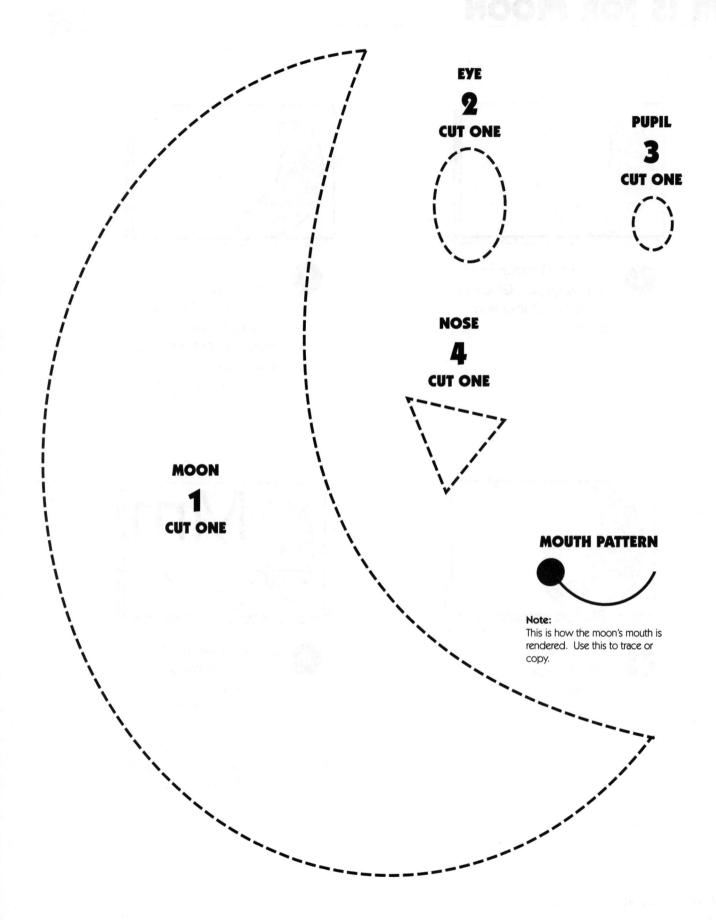

**EYE**

**2**

**CUT ONE**

**PUPIL**

**3**

**CUT ONE**

**NOSE**

**4**

**CUT ONE**

**MOON**

**1**

**CUT ONE**

**MOUTH PATTERN**

**Note:**
This is how the moon's mouth is rendered. Use this to trace or copy.

**Materials:** *black, brown or tan and white paper; scissors; glue; black crayon or marker*

# N IS FOR NEST

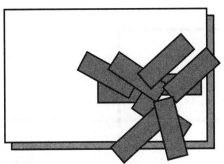

**1** Cut several #1 nest pieces from brown or tan paper. Glue to a sheet of construction paper as illustrated.

**2** Cut three #2 eggs from white paper.
(If you want to make robin eggs, use light blue paper.)
Glue the eggs on top of the completed nest.

**3** Cut the letters *Nn* from construction paper or use the patterns in the back of the book. Glue the letters as shown.

**NEST PIECES**
# 1
**CUT SEVERAL**

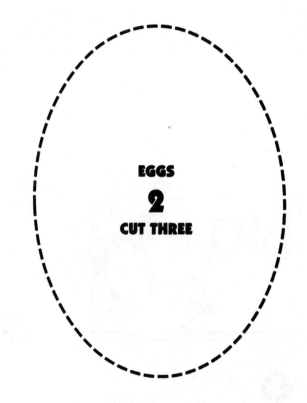

**EGGS**
# 2
**CUT THREE**

**Materials:** *black, brown, dark gray, orange, tan and white paper; scissors; glue; black crayon or marker*

# O IS FOR OWL

**1** Cut one #1 head from tan paper.

**2** Cut two #2 eyes from white or yellow paper and glue to the head. Cut two #3 pupils from black paper and glue on the eyes as shown.

**3** Cut one #4 forehead from tan and glue over part of the eyes, as shown.

**4** Cut one #5 triangle from brown paper and glue to the forehead.

**5** Cut one #6 beak from orange paper and glue in place as shown. Cut three #7 neck feathers from tan paper and glue to the back of the head as illustrated. Glue head to a sheet of construction paper.

**6** Cut the letters *Oo* from construction paper or use the patterns in the back of the book. Glue the letters as shown.

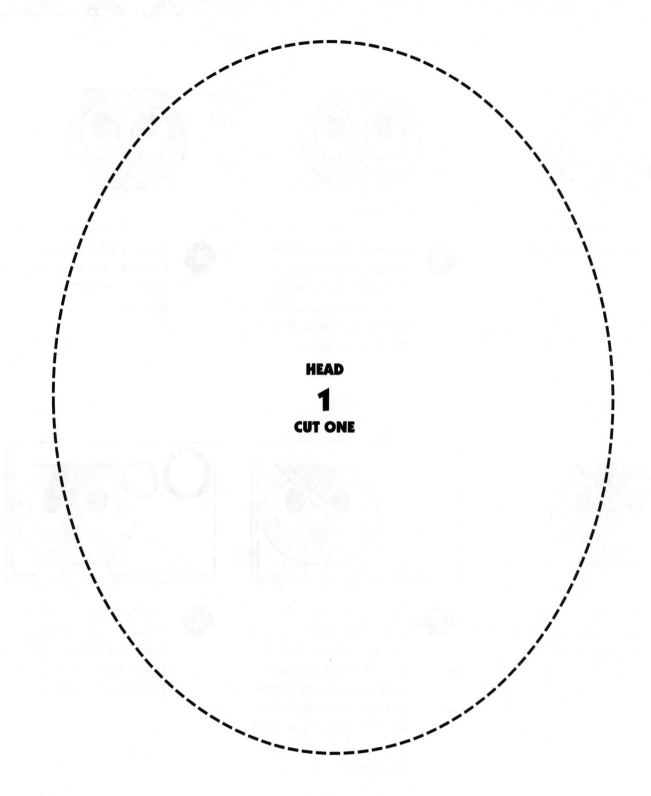

**HEAD**

**1**

**CUT ONE**

# O is for Owl

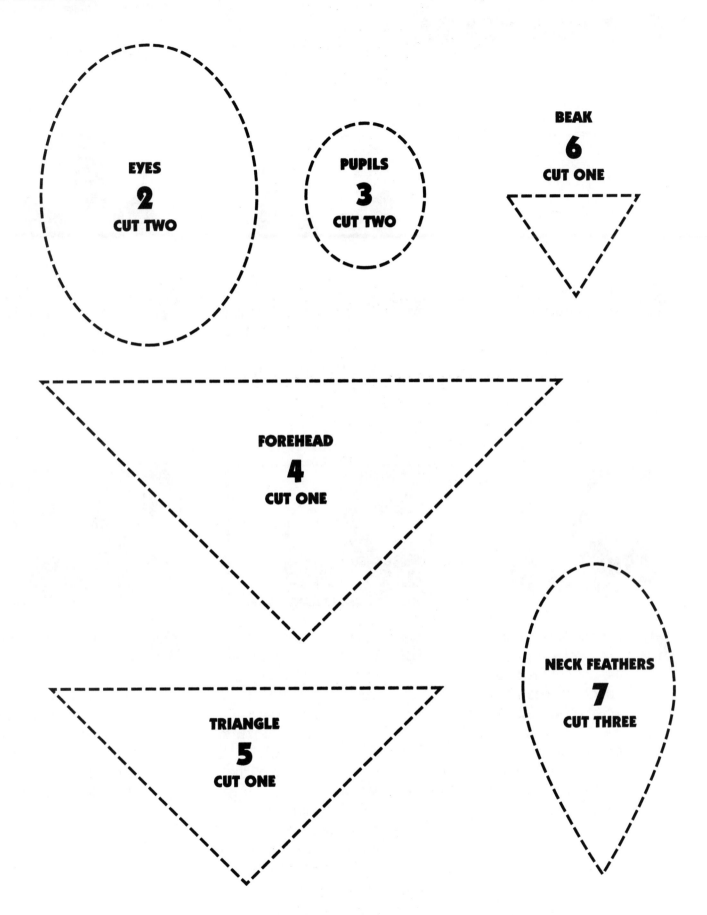

**EYES**
**2**
CUT TWO

**PUPILS**
**3**
CUT TWO

**BEAK**
**6**
CUT ONE

**FOREHEAD**
**4**
CUT ONE

**TRIANGLE**
**5**
CUT ONE

**NECK FEATHERS**
**7**
CUT THREE

# P IS FOR PANDA

**Materials:** *black and white paper; scissors; glue; black crayon or marker*
**Optional Materials:** *wiggly eyes*

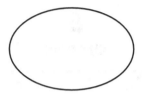

**1** Cut one #1 body from white paper.

**2** Cut four #2 legs and four #3 feet from black paper. Glue the feet to the bottoms of the legs. Then glue the legs to the back of the body as shown.

**3** Cut one #4 stripe from black paper and glue to the upper portion of the body as illustrated.

**4** Cut one #5 tail from black paper and glue to the back of the body. Cut one #6 head from white paper. Cut two #7 ears from black paper and glue to the back of the head as shown. Glue the head on the front of the body.

**5** Cut two #8 eyes from black paper and two #9 eyes from white paper. Cut two #10 pupils from black paper or use a black crayon or marker to draw on the pupils. Glue the #9 eyes on the #8 eyes as shown. Then glue the pupils in the center of the #9 eyes. Now glue the eye pieces to the head as shown. Glue to a sheet of construction paper.

**6** Cut one #11 nose from black paper or use a black crayon or marker to draw on the nose. Cut the letters *Pp* from construction paper or use the patterns in the back of the book. Glue the letters as shown.

**Note:** You may use wiggly eyes.

TLC10114 Copyright © Teaching & Learning Company, Carthage, IL 62321-0010

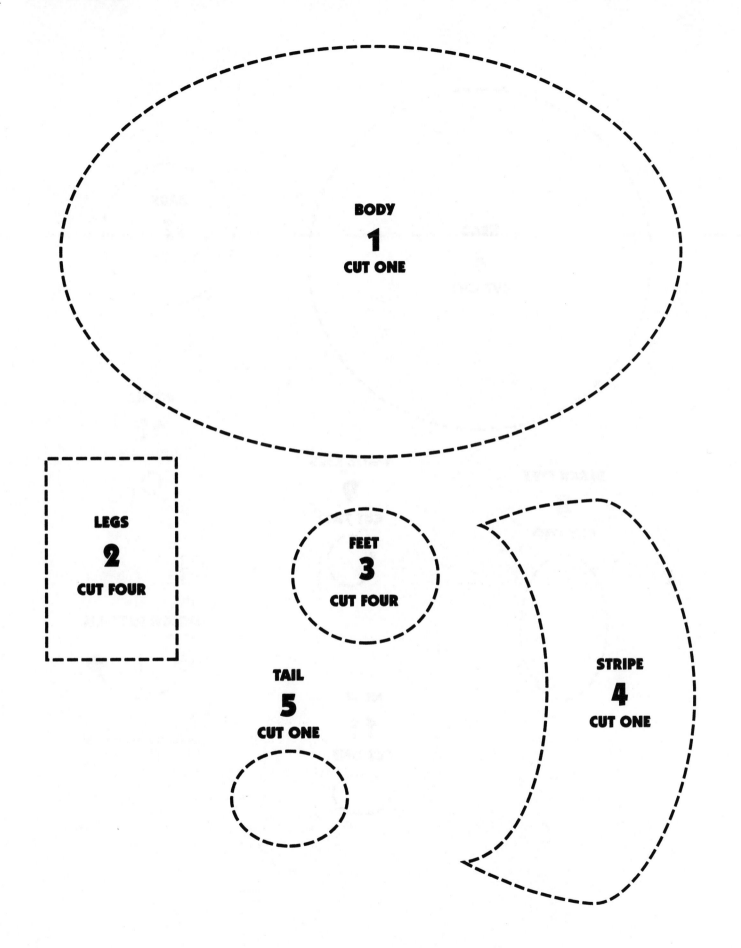

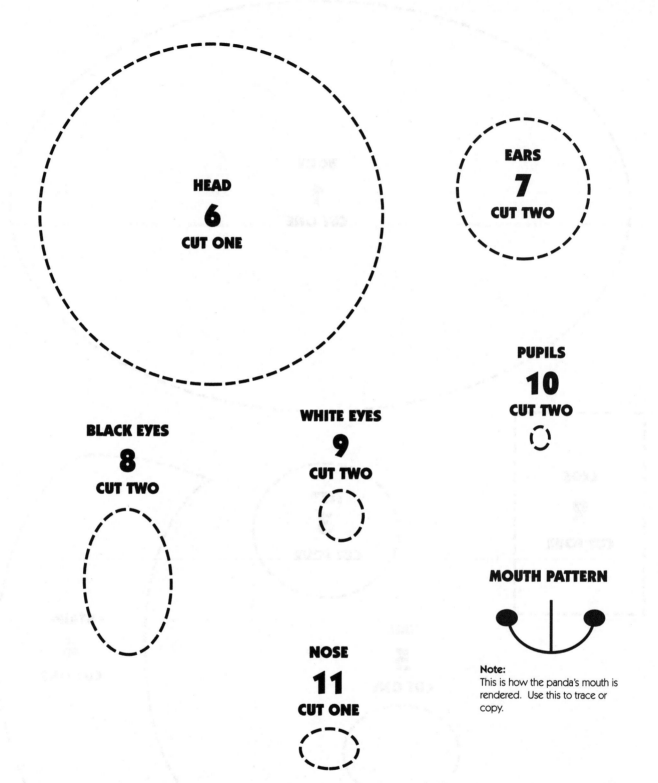

HEAD
**6**
CUT ONE

EARS
**7**
CUT TWO

PUPILS
**10**
CUT TWO

BLACK EYES
**8**
CUT TWO

WHITE EYES
**9**
CUT TWO

MOUTH PATTERN

**Note:**
This is how the panda's mouth is rendered. Use this to trace or copy.

NOSE
**11**
CUT ONE

**Materials:** *multicolored paper, scissors, glue, black crayon or marker*
**Optional Materials:** *stickers, crayons or markers*

# Q IS FOR QUILT

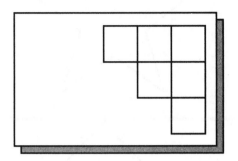

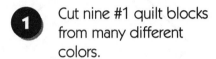

**1** Cut nine #1 quilt blocks from many different colors.

Note: For smaller children, cut one big square and use a marker to draw in the quilt lines.

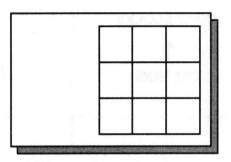

**2** Glue the quilt blocks together to form a big square as shown.

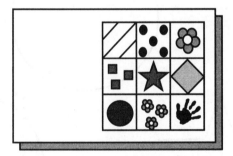

**3** Cut different shapes and glue on the blocks to create your quilt.

**4** Cut the letters *Qq* from construction paper or use the patterns in the back of the book. Glue the letters as shown.

**Note:** A selection of patterns are provided on page 46. If these shapes are too small for your students to cut, try using stickers or crayons and markers to decorate the squares.

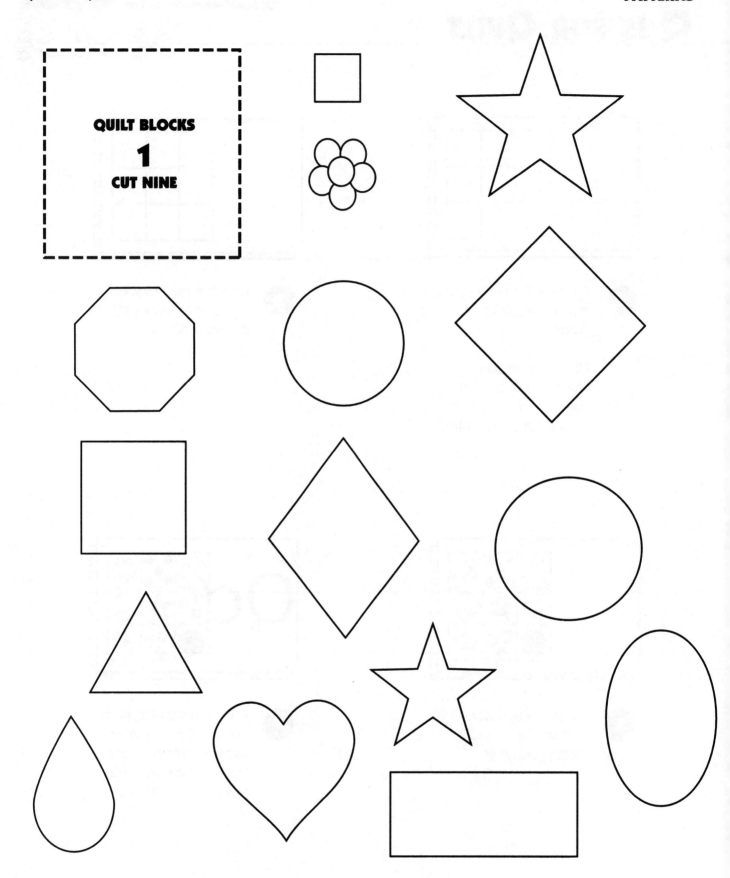

**QUILT BLOCKS**

**1**

**CUT NINE**

**Materials:** *red, orange, yellow, green, blue, purple, violet and white paper; scissors; glue; black crayon or marker*

# R IS FOR RAINBOW

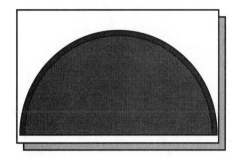

**1** Cut one #1 red arc from red paper. Glue to a sheet of white construction paper.

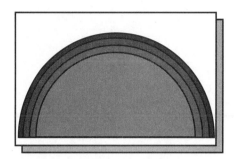

**2** Cut one #2 orange arc from orange paper. Glue on top of the red arc as shown.

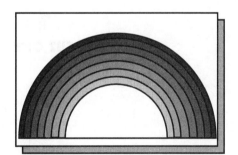

**3** Cut one #3 yellow arc from yellow paper. Glue on top of the orange arc as shown. Cut one #4 green arc from green paper. Glue on top of the yellow arc.

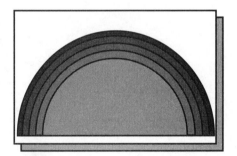

**4** Cut one #5 blue arc from blue paper. Glue on top of the green arc.

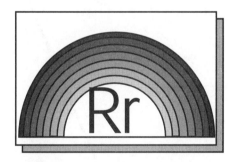

**5** Cut one #6 purple arc from purple paper and glue on top of the blue arc as shown. Cut one #7 violet arc from violet paper. Glue on top of the purple arc as shown. Cut one #8 background from white paper.

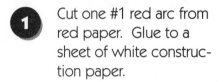

**6** Cut the letters *Rr* from construction paper or use the patterns in the back of the book. Glue the letters as shown.

**Note:** If you use a colored background, use the same color for piece #8.

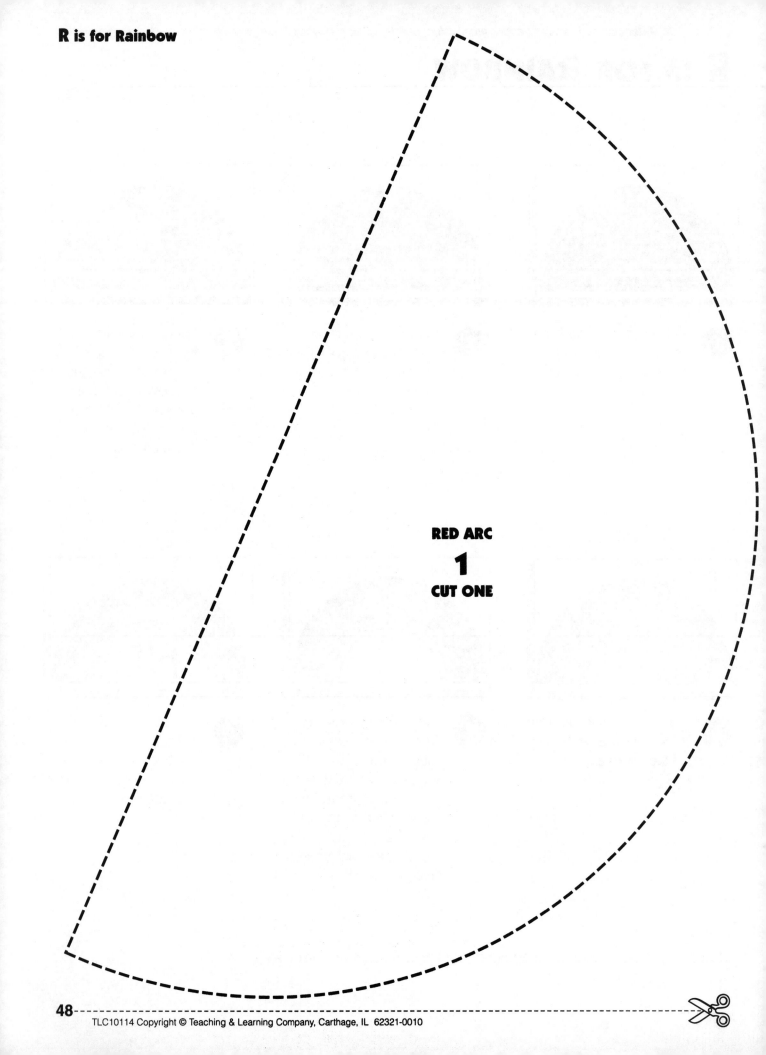

**RED ARC**

**1**

**CUT ONE**

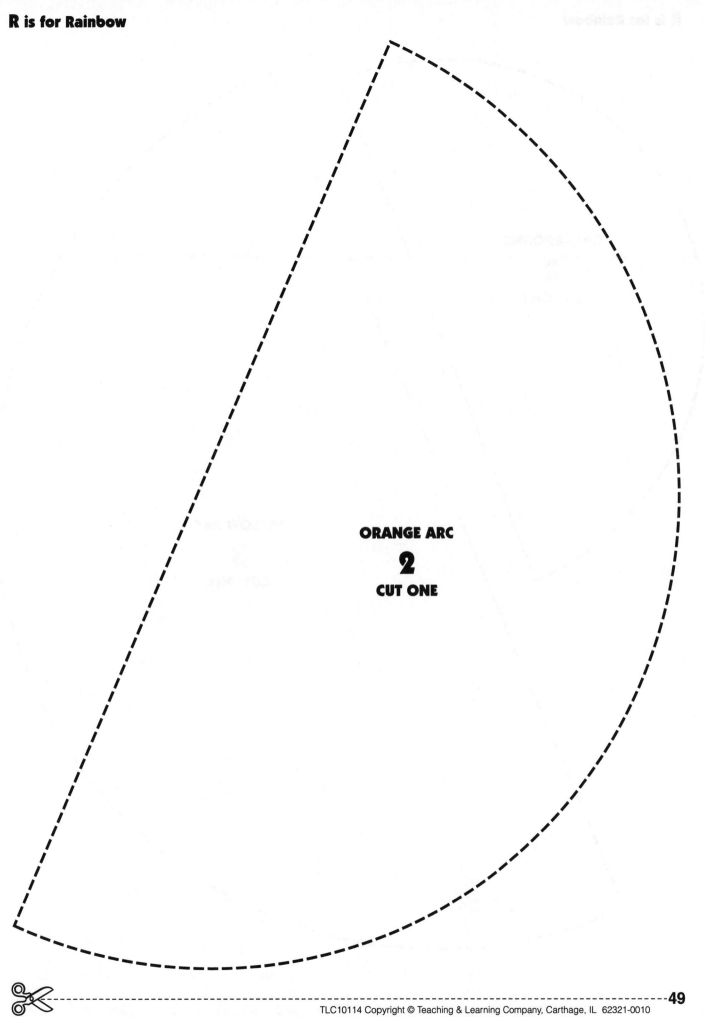

ORANGE ARC

**2**

CUT ONE

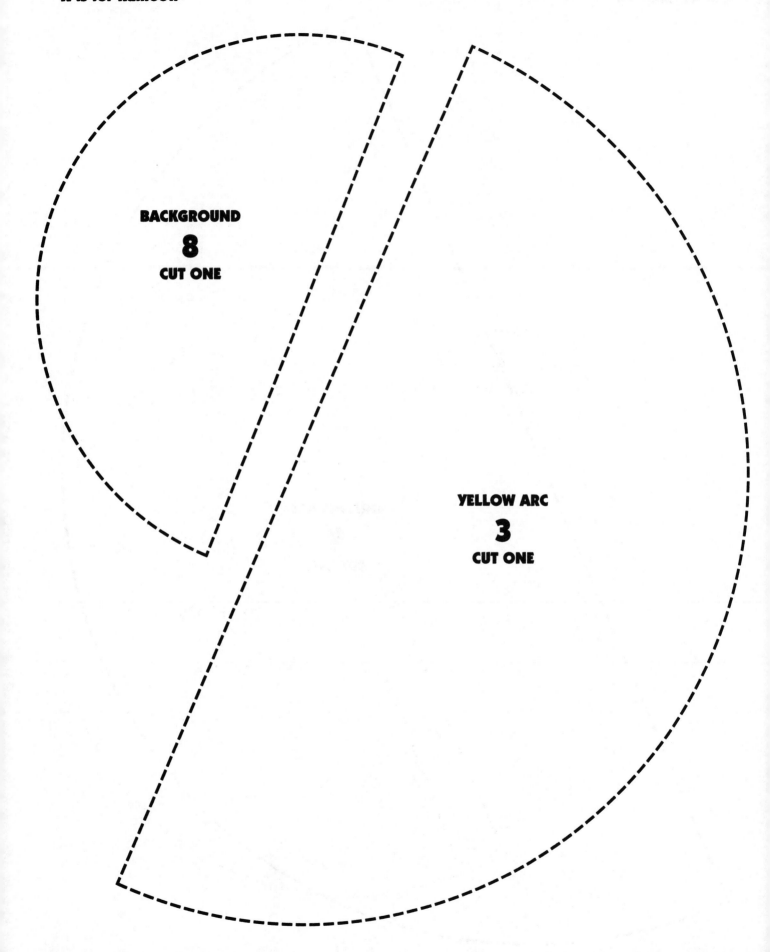

**BACKGROUND**
**8**
**CUT ONE**

**YELLOW ARC**
**3**
**CUT ONE**

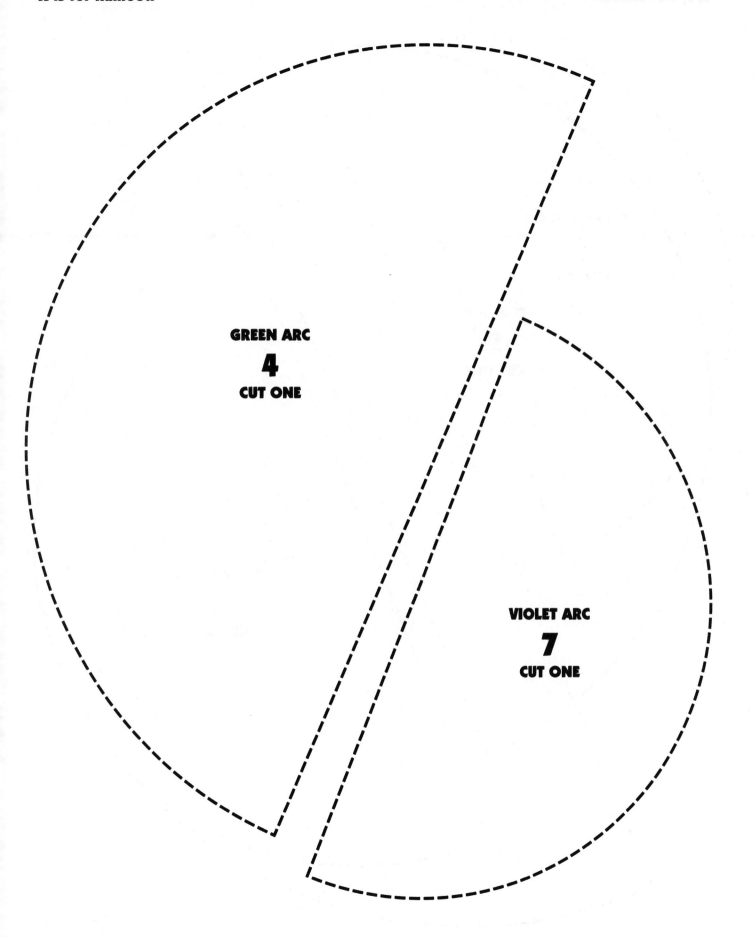

GREEN ARC

**4**

CUT ONE

VIOLET ARC

**7**

CUT ONE

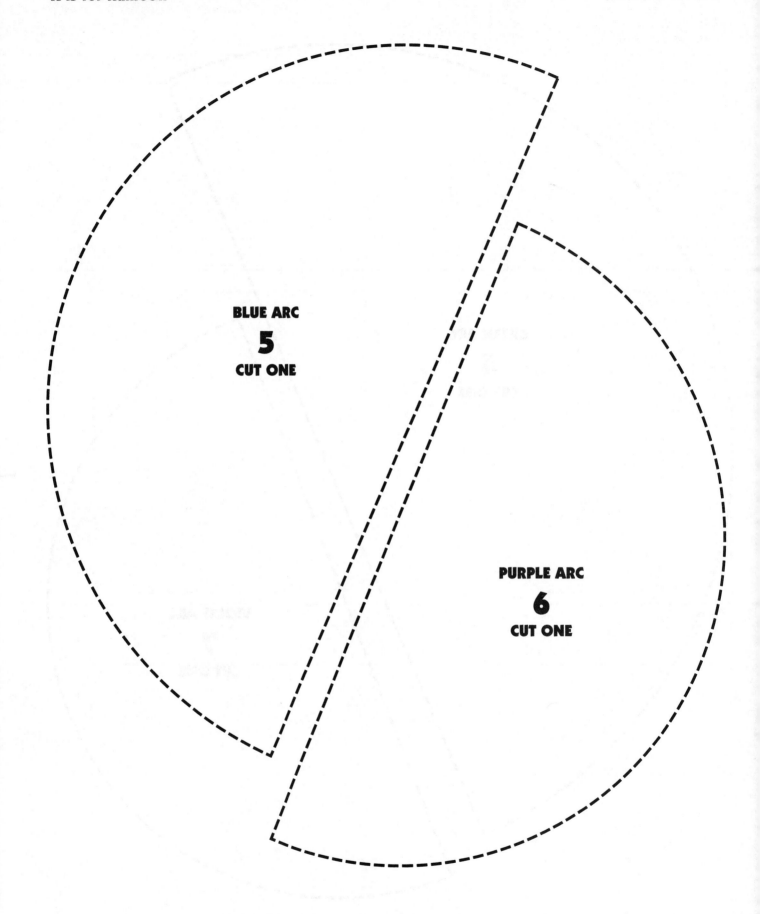

BLUE ARC
**5**
CUT ONE

PURPLE ARC
**6**
CUT ONE

**Materials:** *black, brown, and yellow paper; scissors; glue; black crayon or marker*
**Optional Materials:** *sunflower seeds*

# S IS FOR SUNFLOWER

**1** Cut sixteen #1 petals from yellow paper. Glue eight petals in a circle shape onto a sheet of construction paper.

**2** Glue the remaining eight petals on top of the other petals as shown.

**3** Cut one #2 center from brown paper and glue in the middle of the petals.

**4** Cut several #3 seeds from black paper and glue on the center.

**5** Cut the letters *Ss* from construction paper or use the patterns in the back of the book. Glue the letters as shown.

**Note:** You can glue on real sunflower seeds in the center of the flower.

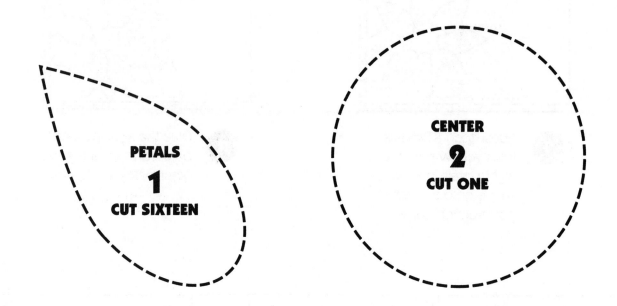

**PETALS**

**1**

**CUT SIXTEEN**

**CENTER**

**2**

**CUT ONE**

**SEEDS**

**3**

**CUT SEVERAL**

**Materials:** brown, tan, and off-white or yellow paper; scissors; glue; black crayon or marker

# T IS FOR TEPEE

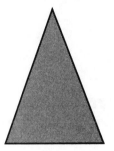

**1** Cut one #1 tepee from tan paper.

**2** Cut one #2 doorway from off-white or yellow paper and glue to the front of the tepee.

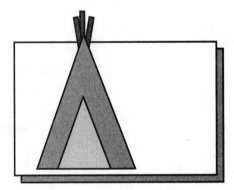

**3** Cut three #3 poles from brown paper. Glue these to the back of the tepee at the top as shown. Glue to a sheet of construction paper.

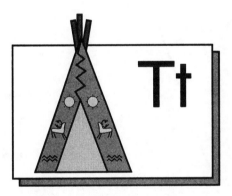

**4** Use a black crayon or marker to decorate your tepee with Native American designs. Cut the letters *Tt* from construction paper or use the patterns in the back of the book. Glue the letters as shown.

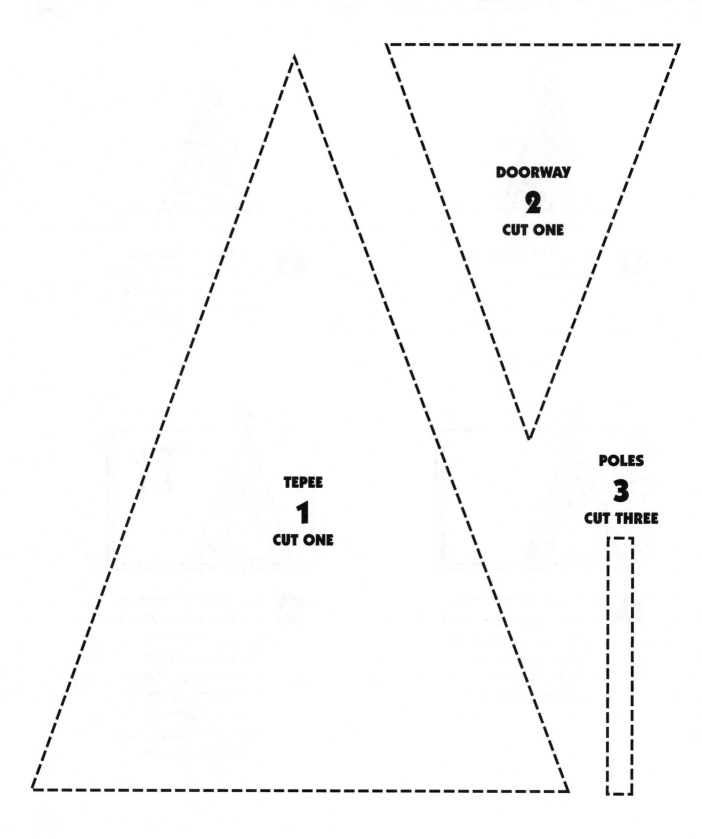

DOORWAY

**2**

CUT ONE

TEPEE

**1**

CUT ONE

POLES

**3**

CUT THREE

**Materials:** *brown, gray and a variety of colors of paper; scissors; glue; black crayon or marker*

# U IS FOR UMBRELLA

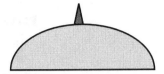

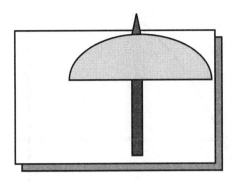

**1** Cut one #1 umbrella from a color of your choice. Cut one #2 top from gray paper and glue to the back of the umbrella at the top as shown.

**2** Cut one #3 pole from gray paper and glue to the back of the umbrella as shown. Glue to a sheet of construction paper.

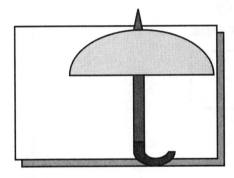

**3** Cut one #4 handle from brown paper and glue to the bottom of the pole.

**4** Draw the pleats in the umbrella with a black crayon or marker as illustrated.
Cut the letters *Uu* from construction paper or use the patterns in the back of the book. Glue the letters as shown.

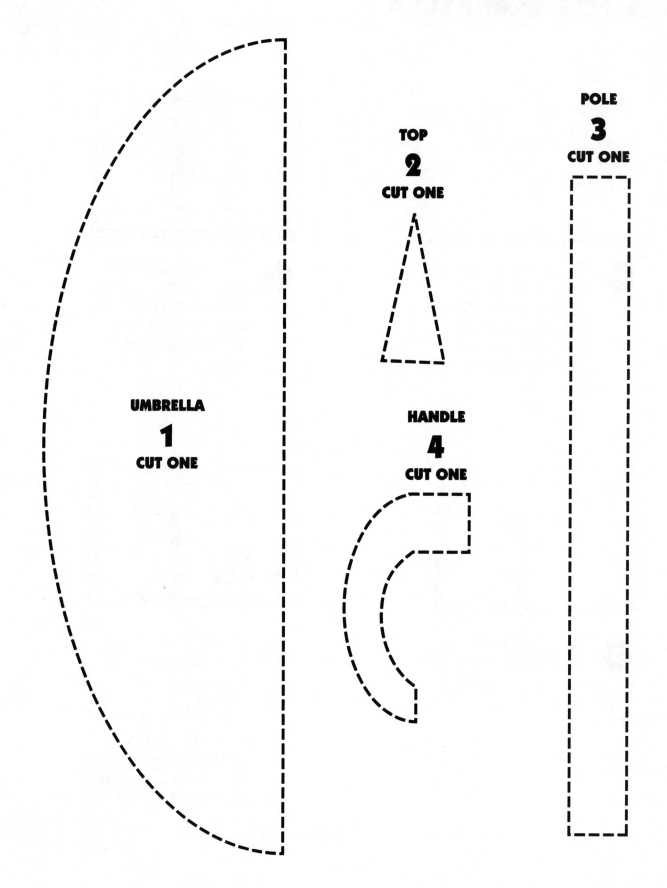

**TOP**
**2**
**CUT ONE**

**POLE**
**3**
**CUT ONE**

**UMBRELLA**
**1**
**CUT ONE**

**HANDLE**
**4**
**CUT ONE**

**Materials:** *violet, dark purple, green and yellow paper; scissors; glue; black crayon or marker*

# V IS FOR VIOLET

**1** Cut five #1 petals from violet paper.
Glue two petals in a heart shape at the top of a sheet of construction paper as shown.

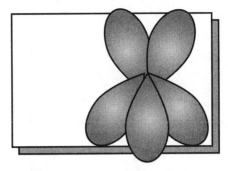

**2** Glue the remaining three petals at the bottom of the page as shown.

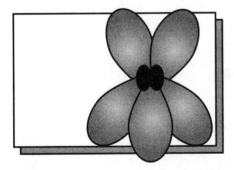

**3** Cut two #2 centers from dark purple, yellow or green paper and glue in place as shown.

**4** Cut the letters *Vv* from construction paper or use the patterns in the back of the book. Glue the letters as shown.

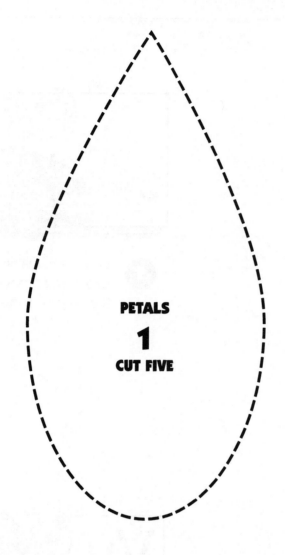

**PETALS**

**1**

**CUT FIVE**

**CENTERS**

**2**

**CUT TWO**

**Materials:** black, dark pink and green paper; scissors; glue; black crayon or marker
**Optional Materials:** watermelon seeds

# W IS FOR WATERMELON

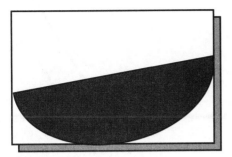

**1** Cut one #1 rind from green paper. Glue to a sheet of construction paper.

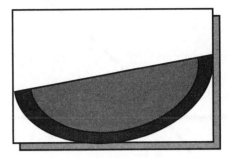

**2** Cut one #2 melon from dark pink paper and glue on top of the green rind as shown.

**3** Cut several #3 seeds from black paper and glue on the melon.

**4** Cut the letters *Ww* from construction paper or use the patterns in the back of the book. Glue the letters as shown.

**Note:** You can use real seeds to glue on the watermelon.

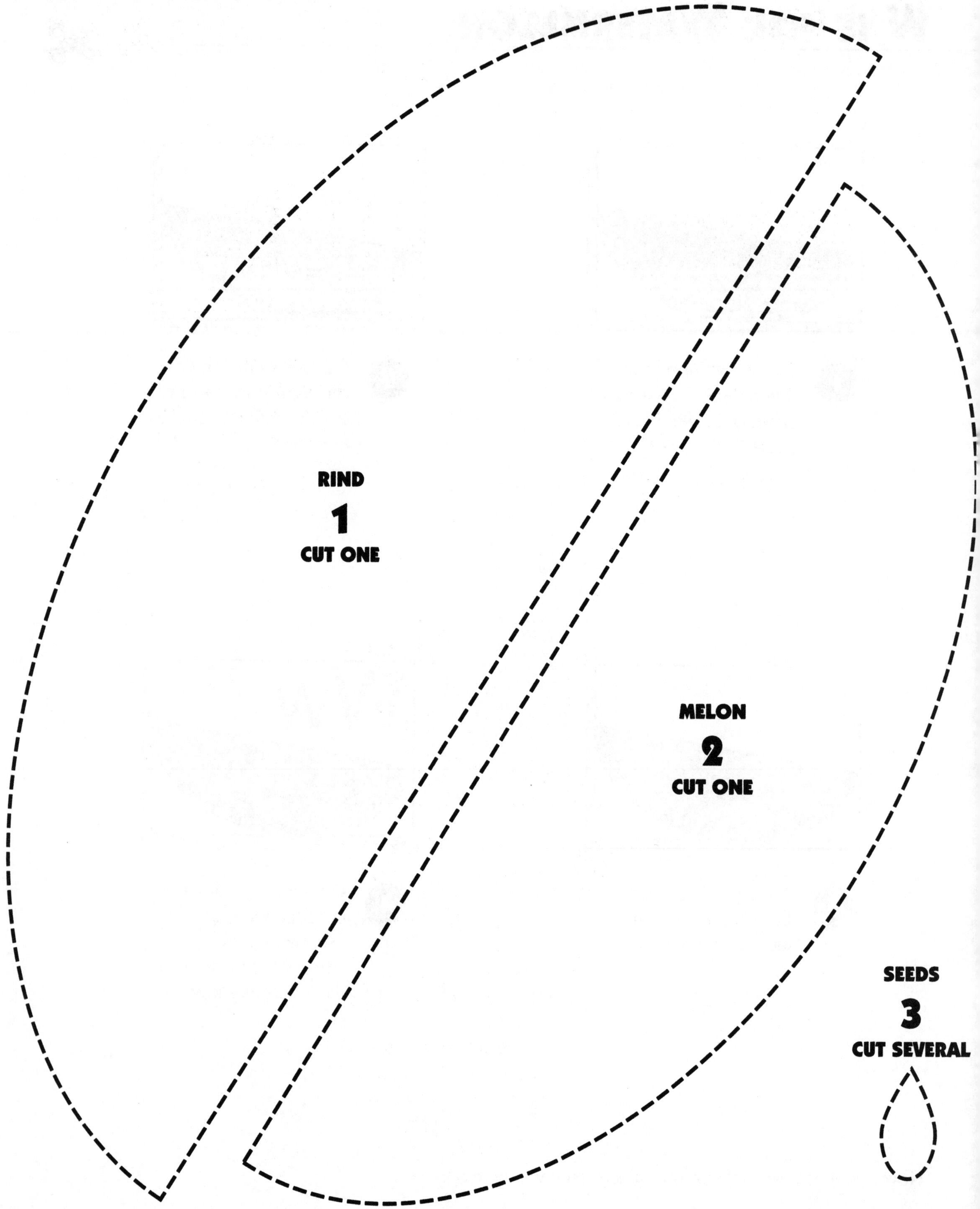

**RIND**

**1**

**CUT ONE**

**MELON**

**2**

**CUT ONE**

**SEEDS**

**3**

**CUT SEVERAL**

*Materials:* a variety of colors of paper, scissors, glue, black crayon or marker

# X IS FOR XYLOPHONE

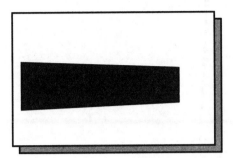

**1** Cut one #1 base from a color of your choice. Glue to a sheet of construction paper.

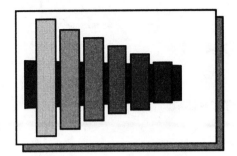

**2** Cut one each of #2, #3, #4, #5, #6 and #7 crossbars from rainbow colors. Glue the cross-bars to the base from largest to smallest as shown.

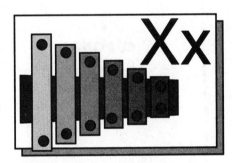

**3** Cut twelve #8 circles from gray or black paper and glue one on each side of each crossbar as shown.
Note: You can use a black crayon or marker to draw these.
Cut the letters *Xx* from construction paper or use the patterns in the back of the book. Glue the letters as shown.

**CIRCLES**

**8**

**CUT TWELVE**

**BASE**

**1**

**CUT ONE**

**RED CROSSBAR**

**2**

**CUT ONE**

**ORANGE CROSSBAR**

**3**

**CUT ONE**

**YELLOW CROSSBAR**

**4**

**CUT ONE**

**GREEN CROSSBAR**

**5**

**CUT ONE**

**BLUE CROSSBAR**

**6**

**CUT ONE**

**PURPLE CROSSBAR**

**7**

**CUT ONE**

# Y IS FOR YO-YO

**Materials:** *black and a variety of colors of paper, scissors, glue, black crayon or marker*
**Optional Materials:** *yarn*

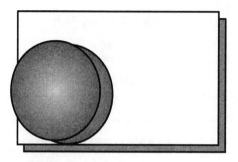

**1** Cut two #1 yo-yos from a color of your choice. Glue the two circles as shown. Glue to a sheet of construction paper.

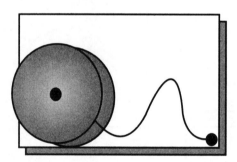

**2** Cut a piece of yarn or use a black crayon or marker to draw a string. Draw or glue in place as shown. Cut two #2 buttons from black paper and glue one to the center of the yo-yo and the other to the end of the string.

**3** Cut the letters *Yy* from construction paper or use the patterns in the back of the book. Glue the letters as shown.

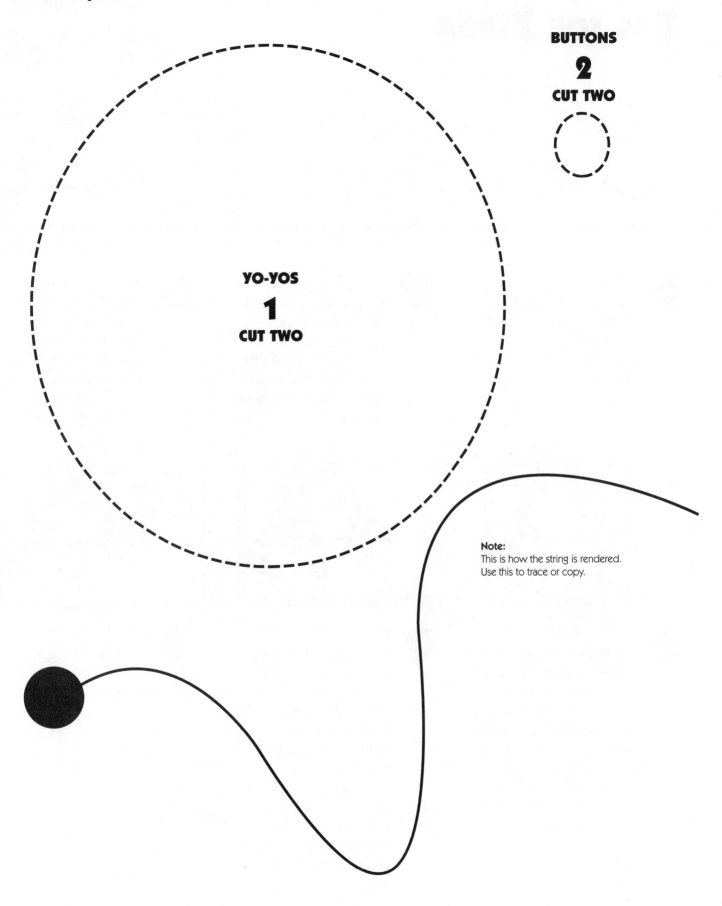

**BUTTONS**

**2**

**CUT TWO**

**YO-YOS**

**1**

**CUT TWO**

**Note:**
This is how the string is rendered.
Use this to trace or copy.

**Materials:** black, brown and white paper; scissors; glue; black crayon or marker

# Z IS FOR ZEBRA

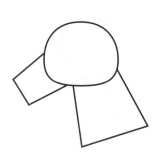

**1** Cut one #1 snout, one #2 head and one #3 neck from white paper. Glue the snout and neck to the back of the head as shown.

**2** Cut one #4 nose from white paper and glue to the snout as shown. Cut two #5 ears from white paper. Glue one to the back of the head. Note: Save the other ear for later.

**3** Cut several #6 mane hairs from black paper. Glue three to the top of the head. Glue the rest down the back of the head and neck as shown. Glue to a sheet of construction paper.

**4** Now glue the second #5 ear to the head as illustrated. Cut one #7 inner ear from black paper and glue to the center of the front ear. Cut one #8 eye from white paper and glue on the head. Cut one #9 pupil from black paper and glue in the center of the eye or use a black crayon or marker to draw on the pupil.

**5** Cut two #10 nostrils from black paper and glue on the nose. Cut four #11 face stripes from black paper. Glue three on the nose and one on the top of the neck. Cut three #12 head stripes from black paper and glue on the head as shown. Cut three #13 neck stripes from black paper and glue on the neck as shown.

**6** Cut the letters *Zz* from construction paper or use the patterns in the back of the book. Glue the letters as shown.

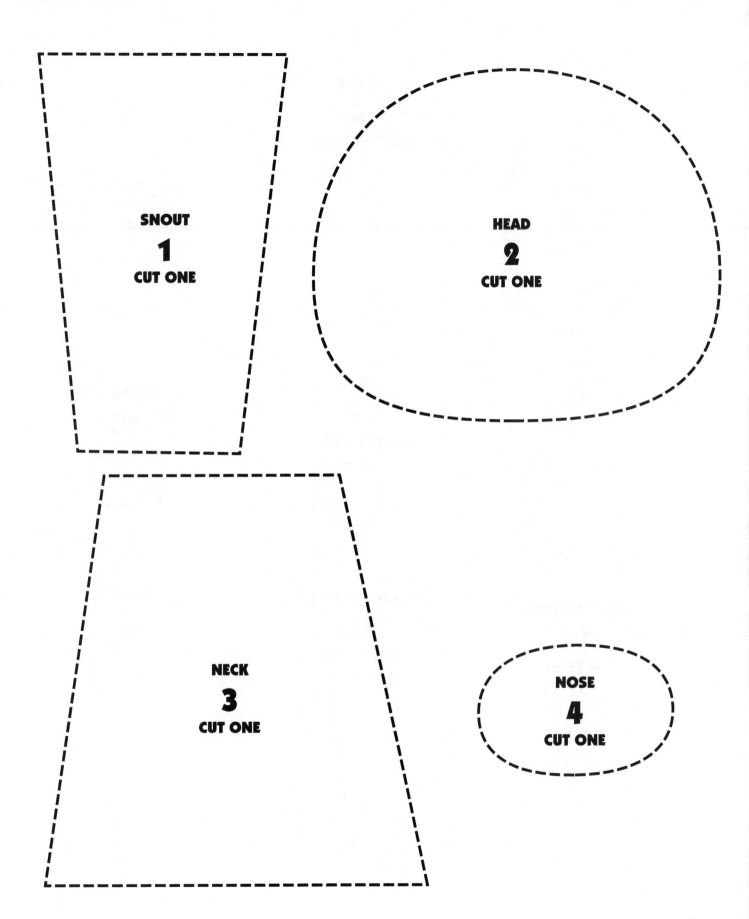

**SNOUT**
**1**
CUT ONE

**HEAD**
**2**
CUT ONE

**NECK**
**3**
CUT ONE

**NOSE**
**4**
CUT ONE

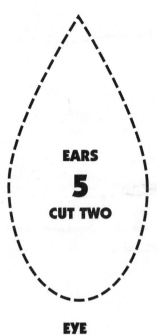

**EARS**

**5**

**CUT TWO**

**MANE**

**6**

**CUT SEVERAL**

**INNER EAR**

**7**

**CUT ONE**

**EYE**

**8**

**CUT ONE**

**PUPIL**

**9**

**CUT ONE**

**NOSTRILS**

**10**

**CUT TWO**

**NECK STRIPES**

**11**

**CUT THREE**

**HEAD STRIPES**

**12**

**CUT THREE**

**FACE STRIPES**

**13**

**CUT FOUR**

Aa

Cc

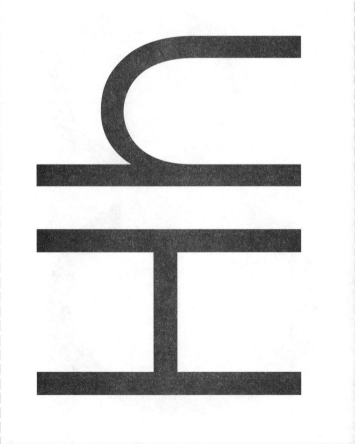

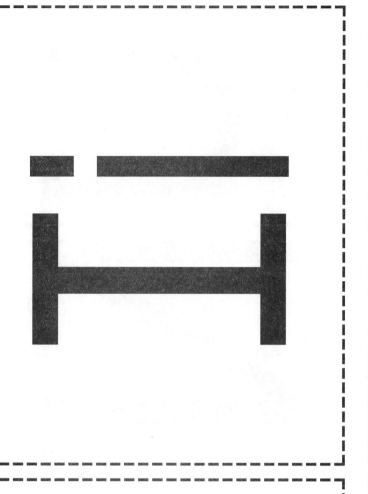

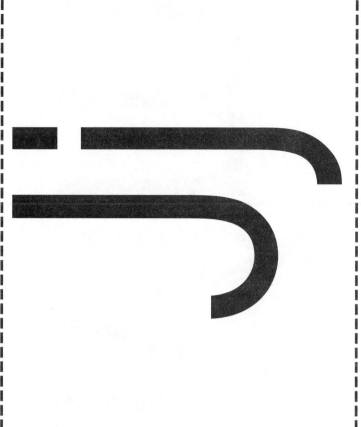

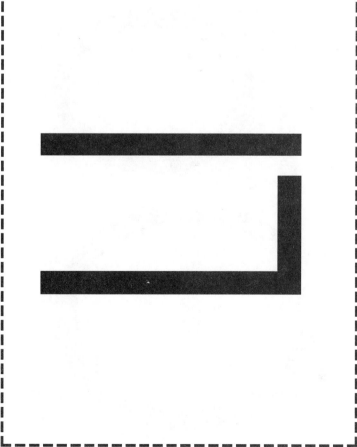

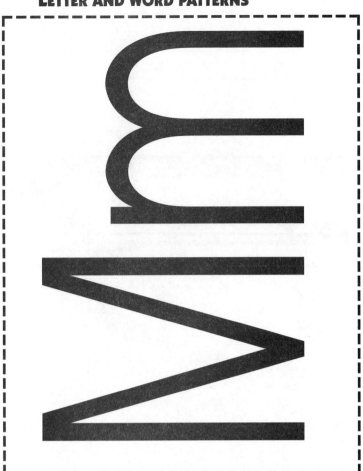

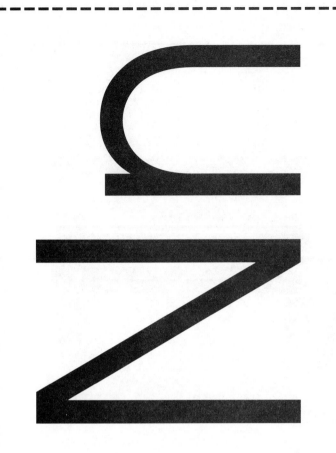

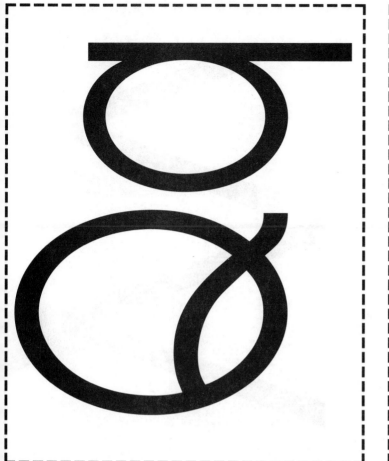

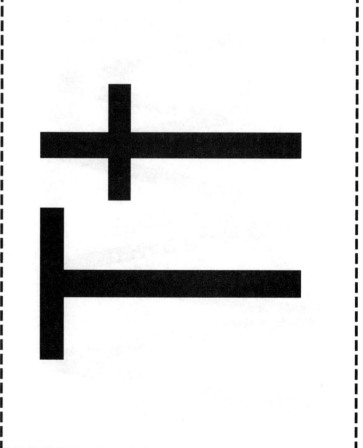

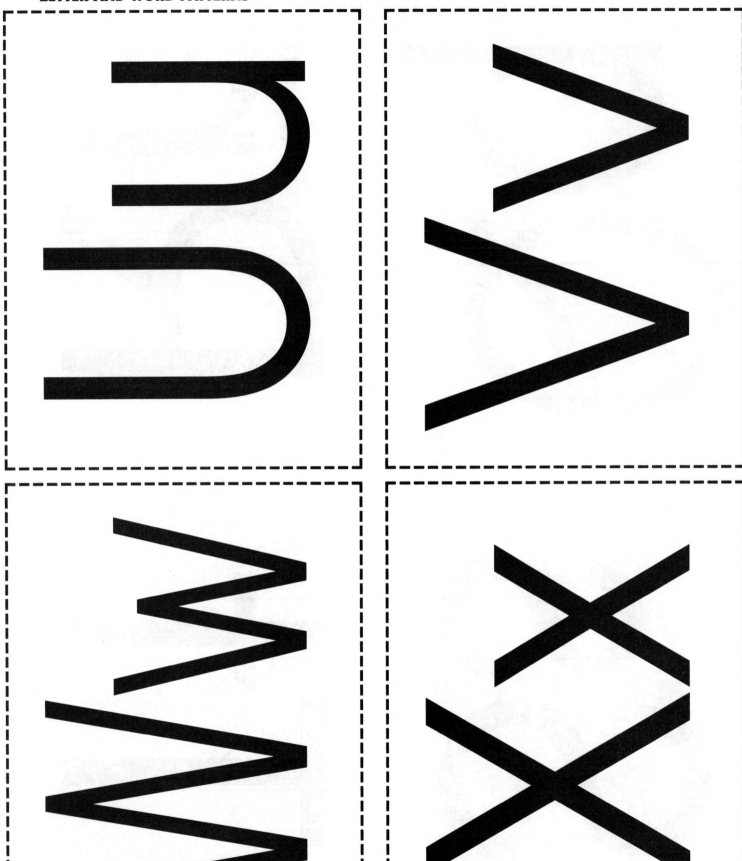

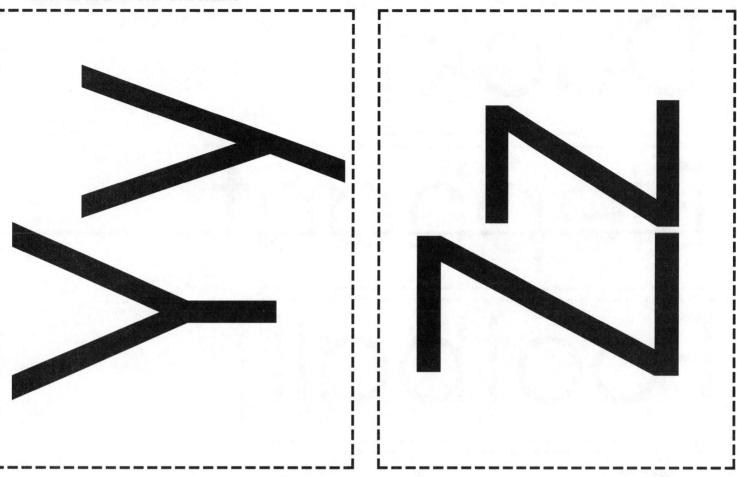

Apple

Baby

Camera

Duck

Elephant

Football

Goat

House          Igloo

Jack-in-the-Box

# Kite

## Lollipops

# Moon

# Nest  Owl

# Panda  Quilt

# Rainbow

# Sunflower

## Tepee   Vest

## Umbrella

## Watermelon

## Xylophone

## Yo-yo   Zebra